Contents

KU-040-157

Introduction   4

Pronunciation guide   6

1 ahlan wa sahlan   7
saying hello
... and goodbye
introducing yourself
... and getting to know people

Arabic script: introduction   15

2 min wayn inta?   17
talking about where you're from
... and your nationality
saying where you live
giving your phone number

Arabic script: 1   25

Arabic script: 2   26

3 haadi Farida   27
introducing friends and family
talking about yourself and your
   family
saying what you do for a living
saying how old you are

Arabic script: 3   35

Arabic script: 4   36

4 waaHid 'ahwa, min faDlak   37
ordering tea and coffee
... and other drinks
offering, accepting, refusing
asking and paying for the bill

Checkpoint 1   45

5 law samaHt, fiih maT9am
hawn?   49
asking what there is
... and whereabouts it is
finding out which days places are
   open
... and what time they're open

Arabic script: 5   57

Arabic script: 6   58

6 kiif aruuH lis-suu'?   59
asking the way
... and following directions
making enquiries
... and getting help to understand

Arabic script: 7   67

Arabic script: the hamza   68

7 'addaysh haada?   69
asking for what you want
understanding the price
shopping in a market
bargaining

Checkpoint 2   77

8 9andak ghurfa?   81
finding a suitable hotel room
... and saying how long you want
   to stay
checking in at the hotel
making requests

Arabic script: numbers   89

Arabic script: answers   90

9 fiih qiTaar li Halab?   91
saying where you're going
asking about public transport
buying tickets
checking travel times

Modern Standard Arabic   99

10 il-akl laziiz!   101
understanding the menu
saying what you like and what
   you don't like
ordering a meal
expressing appreciation

Checkpoint 3   109

Transcripts and answers   113

Grammar   134

Arabic–English glossary   140

Introduction

Welcome to **Talk Arabic**, BBC Active's new course for absolute beginners. It consists of a book and two 60-minute CDs recorded by native Arabic speakers.

Designed for adults, learning at home or in a class, **Talk Arabic** is the ideal introduction to Arabic, covering the basic everyday language for a visit to an Arabic-speaking country, whether for work or on holiday. It is suitable for a first level qualification, such as the Breakthrough level of the national Languages Ladder.

Modern Standard Arabic (MSA), which is the formal language of the broadcast media, the press and literature, is not used for everyday informal conversations and transactions. **Talk Arabic** has therefore chosen to focus on the Arabic of the Levant, spoken in Lebanon, Syria, Jordan and Palestine and widely understood elsewhere. It is not too far removed from MSA, and some of the main differences are highlighted on pages 99-100.

A great advantage of learning Levantine Arabic is that it can be learnt to a reasonable level without having to master the complex Arabic script. To enable you to make faster progress in speaking Arabic, **Talk Arabic** presents the sounds of Arabic using the script used for English and other western languages (known as roman script). The basics of Arabic script are also introduced within self-contained sections of the book.

Talk Arabic encourages you to make genuine progress and promotes a real sense of achievement. The key to its effectiveness lies in its systematic approach. Key features include:

- simple step-by-step presentation of new language
- involvement and interaction at every stage of the learning process
- useful language learning strategies
- regular progress checks
- reference section, including guide to pronunciation, grammar summary, audio transcripts and glossary

Acknowledgements
BBC Active would like to thank everyone who contributed to this course. Our particular thanks go to Leslie McLoughlin of Exeter University and Ruba Jurdi Associates.

How to use Talk Arabic

Wherever you see this: **1·5**, the phrases or dialogues are recorded on the CD (i.e. CD1, track 5).

Each of the 10 units is completed in 10 easy-to-follow steps.

1   Read the first page of the unit to focus on what you're aiming to learn and to set your learning in context. Then follow steps 2 to 5 for each of the next four pages of the unit.

2   Listen to the key words and phrases – don't be tempted to read them first. Then listen to them again, this time reading them in your book too. Finally, try reading them out loud before listening one more time.

3   Work your way, step by step, through the activities. These highlight key language elements and are carefully designed to develop your listening skills and your understanding of Arabic. You can check your answers in *Transcripts and answers* starting on page 113.

4   Read the **bil 9arabi** explanations of how Arabic works as you come to them. Wherever you see **G00** these are developed further in the *Grammar* section at the back of the book.

5   After completing the activities, close your book and listen to the conversations straight through. The more times you listen, the more familiar and comfortable you'll become with the sounds of Arabic. You might also like to read the transcripts at this stage.

6   Complete the consolidation activities on the *Put it all together* page, checking your answers with the *Transcripts and answers*.

7   Use the language you've just learnt. The audio presenters will prompt you and guide you through the *Now you're talking!* page as you practise speaking Arabic.

8   Check your progress. First, test your knowledge with the *quiz*. Then check whether you can do everything on the *checklist* – if in doubt, go back and spend some more time on the relevant section. You'll have further opportunities to check your progress in the strategic *Checkpoints* after units 4, 7 and 10.

9   Read the learning strategy at the end of the unit, which provides ideas for consolidating and extending what you've learnt.

10 Finally, relax and listen to the whole unit, understanding what the people are saying in Arabic and taking part in the conversations. This time you may not need to have the book to hand.

Pronunciation guide

Talk Arabic presents the sounds of Levantine Arabic using roman script, i.e. the same script as English. This is called transliteration. In Arabic script capital letters aren't used for places, and so the transliteration will reflect the actual sounds e.g. **bayruut** *Beirut* , **Halab** *Aleppo*. It does, however, show all names with initial capitals in order to distinguish them from general vocabulary e.g. **Mona**, **Zeinab**, **Sami**.

Vowels

The vowel sounds are represented as:

a	i	u	aa	ii	uu	aw	ay
c<u>a</u>t	b<u>i</u>n	p<u>u</u>t	c<u>a</u>r	b<u>ee</u>n	p<u>oo</u>l	c<u>ow</u>	d<u>ay</u>

Consonants

Many consonants sound much as they do in English but there are a few extra sounds in Arabic:

- The capital letters **D**, **DH**, **S**, **T** are used to show 'heavier' versions of **d**, **dh**, **s**, **t**. Listen out for them on the audio to hear exactly how they're pronounced. **H** is a breathy **h** as if breathing on glasses to clean them.

  r is more rolled than in English

  gh sounds like a French r, or a gargling sound

  j sounds like the soft s of lei<u>s</u>ure

  kh sounds like the ch of Lo<u>ch</u> Ness

  q and **'** have two sounds: either the hard ck in knu<u>ck</u>le or the cockney glottal stop in bu'er (butter)

  9 is used because there's no English equivalent of the sound it represents, which is similar to a strangled ah sound made by narrowing the throat.

- Where the transliteration shows a double consonant these must both be pronounced to give a long sound, such as **sayyaara** *car*, which is pronounced **say-yaara**.

- There is no v or p sound. As a rule they become **b**, e.g. **suubermarket**.

Stress

Most Arabic words are stressed, and this varies from dialect to dialect. Generally it falls on the last but one syllable in a word:

shuu <u>is</u>mak? *What's your name?*   **wayn <u>saa</u>kin?** *Where do you live?*

ahlan wa sahlan

saying hello

... and goodbye

introducing yourself

... and getting to know people

In Arabic-speaking countries greetings and social pleasantries are very important and a wide variety exist. Most greetings have a set reply, so it's useful to learn each greeting as a pair. If someone says **marHaba** *hello*, for example, the response is **marHabtayn** literally *two hellos*.

Alongside **marHaba** the most widely used greetings are **is-salaam 9alaykum** *may peace be upon you*, **ahlan wa sahlan** *hello*, and **ahlan** *hi*.

is-salaam 9alaykum is a little more formal and often heard when one person greets a number of people at the same time. **ahlan wa sahlan** means *welcome* as well as *hello*, and is used in particular when someone welcomes you into their home.

Greetings and welcomes will be repeated several times throughout an initial conversation, the more times the better.

Saying hello

1   **1•2** Listen to the key language:

is-salaam 9alaykum.	May peace be upon you.
wa 9alaykum is-salaam.	*reply*: And upon you be peace.
ahlan wa sahlan.	Hello./Welcome.
ahlan fiik/ahlan fiiki.	*reply*: Hello. (to m/f)
ahlan.	Hi./Hello.
kiif il-Haal?	How are you?
bi-khayr, shukran.	Well, thank you.
il-Hamdullilaah.	Praise be to God.
w-inta/w-inti?	And you? (to m/f)

2   **1•3** Listen as Hiba Mustafa, the receptionist at the Umayyad Hotel greets people. Which greetings does she use?

---

bil 9arabi In Arabic …

when you greet someone you know well, you can use **ya** in front of their name:

ahlan ya Ahmad. *Hi Ahmad*. **ahlan ya Mona.** *Hi Mona*.

In a more formal setting, such as at work or in a hotel, you can use **ya** with someone's title:

is-salaam 9alaykum ya madaam Fawziyya/ya sayyid Salih/ya aanisa Hoda. *Hello Mrs Fawziyya/Mr Salih/Miss Hoda*.

---

3   **1•4** Later Mr Hamdi meets Mrs Fawziyya in the hotel lobby. Tick the key phrases above in the order which you hear them.

4   **1•5** Listen as two friends greet each other:

- How does MuHsin greet Mona? ....
- How does Mona reply? ....

... and goodbye

1 **1•6** Listen to the key language:

SabaaH il-khayr.	Good morning.
SabaaH in-nuur.	*reply*: Good morning.
masaa il-khayr.	Good evening.
masaa in-nuur.	*reply*: Good evening.
ma9a as-salaama.	Goodbye.
allaah yisalmak/yisalmik.	*reply*: Goodbye. (to m/f) *Lit*. May God bless you.
ashuufak/ashuufik ba9dayn.	See you later. (to m/f)

2 **1•7** Listen to Hiba Mustafa saying hello and goodbye to the following guests at the Umayyad Hotel and match them with the above phrases.

Mrs Fawziyya ....   Miss Hoda ....

Mr Hamdi ....   Mr Haddad ....

---

bil 9arabi In Arabic ...

the words for *you* in sentences like *God bless you* or *See you later* are **-ak** for a man and **-ik** for a woman. They go at the end of the verb:

ashuufak *I see you* (m)   **allaah yisalmak** *God bless you* (m)

ashuufik *I see you* (f)   **allaah yisalmik** *God bless you* (f)

---

3 **1•8** Listen to Mrs Fawziyya talking to some people. Circle m if she's talking to a man or f for a woman. You will hear **kiif Haalak?** which is another way of saying *How are you?*

1 m f   2 m f   3 m f   4 m f   5 m f

4 Now try the following. How would you:

- say *good morning* to your friend Rania?
- reply when a man says goodbye to you?
- say *see you later* to a female colleague?

Introducing yourself

1   **1•9** Listen to the key language:

ana ...	I am ...
inta/inti ...?	Are you ...? (to m/f) *informal*
HaDirtak/HaDirtik ...?	Are you ...? (to m/f) *formal*
aywa, ana ...	Yes, I am ...
laa', ana mish ...	No, I'm not ...
law samaHt/law samaHti.	Excuse me. (to m/f)

2   **1•10** Mona is waiting for Muhsin's colleagues to show up. She hasn't met them before. Listen and tick the four people she's looking for.

Jamal   Lutfi   Nureddine   Mustafa   Zeinab   Samia

---

bil 9arabi In Arabic ...

there are no words for *am*, *is*, *are* – if you want to say *I am*, *you are*, *he is* etc. you just use *I*, *you*, *he*, etc. on their own:

ana *I/I am*

inta *you/you are* (m)   **inti** *you/you are* (f)
huwwa *he/he is*   **hiyya** *she/she is*

ana Mona *I'm Mona*; **huwwa Jamal** *He's Jamal*; **hiyya Farida** *She's Farida*.

In simple spoken sentences like these, *not* is **mish**:
ana mish Mona *I'm not Mona*.   **G8**

---

3   **1•11** A number of delegates are checking in at a conference in Cairo and introducing themselves. Listen and fill in the gaps:

- ⚫ .... **HaDirtak Mustafa Amin?**
- ◆ .... **ana Mustafa Amin, wa ....?**
- ⚫ **ana Adnan Hasan.**
- ◆ **ahlan wa sahlan. .... Mustafa Amin. .... Dalia Mustafa?**
- ⚫ **laa', ... Dalia Mustafa, ana Amira Ahmad!**
- ◆ **ahlan, ya Amira!**

... and getting to know people

1   1•12 Listen to the key language:

shuu ismak/ismik?	What's your name? (to m/f)
ismi ...	My name is ...
tasharrafna.	Pleased to meet you. *Lit*. We have been honoured.
ish-sharaf ili.	*reply*: The pleasure is mine. *Lit*. The honour is mine.

---

bil 9arabi In Arabic ...

to say *my*, you add **-i** to the noun you're talking about: **ism** *name*, **ismi** *my name*.

To say *your*, you add **-ak** or **-ik**: **ismak** *your name* (m), **ismik** *your name* (f).
                                                                                    G5

---

2   1•13 There's a wedding reception at the Hotel Umayyad. Listen to a conversation between Sami Suleiman and Nadia Rif'at and tick these phrases as you hear them. Which phrase is left over?

ismi ...	**ahlan fiik**
ish-sharaf ili	**shuu ismik?**
shuu ismak?	**tasharrafna**

3   1•14 At the Umayyad Hotel bar guests are finding out each other's names. Listen and complete the first part of the conversation:

- **ahlan wa sahlan.** ....?
- ◆ ...... **Zeinab,** .... ?
- **ismi Ahmad,** ....?

4   1•15 Sami is introduced to some more people. Listen and number the replies in the order he says them.

a **marHabtayn, shuu ismik?**
b **bi-khayr il-Hamdullilaah.**
c **ahlan fiik ismi Sami.**
d **ish-sharaf ili. w-inta shuu ismak?**

put it **all together**

1 Match the English with the Arabic phrases:

a	How are you?	1	**tasharrafna.**
b	Pleased to meet you.	2	**ashuufak ba9dayn.**
c	May peace be upon you.	3	**marHabtayn.**
d	Good evening. (reply)	4	**SabaaH il-khayr.**
e	Well, thank you.	5	**masaa in-nuur.**
f	Hello. (reply)	6	**ahlan wa sahlan.**
g	Hello. (welcome)	7	**kiif il-Haal?**
h	See you later. (to m)	8	**is-salaam 9alaykum.**
i	Good morning.	9	**bi-khayr shukran.**

2 What could these people be saying to each other?

a  b

c  d

3 How would you ....

a say *hi* to your friend, Ahmad?
b reply to a man who greeted you with **ahlan wa sahlan**?
c ask Farida *and you, how are you?*

now you're talking!

1   **1•16** Answer as if you were Barbara Cox, on holiday in Damascus. A fellow guest greets you in the hotel lobby.

- **masaa il-khayr.**
- ◆ Greet him appropriately.
- **ahlan wa sahlan, ana ismi Nabiil. shuu ismik?**
- ◆ Reply to the greeting, and introduce yourself.
- **tasharrafna.**
- ◆ Reply accordingly.

2   **1•17** Nabiil introduces you to his wife.

- ◆ Say that you're pleased to meet her and ask her how she is.
- **bi-khayr, shukran. il-Hamdullilaah. wa HaDirtik?**
- ◆ Say you're well, thank you.
- **ma9a as-salaama. ashuufik ba9dayn.**
- ◆ Reply accordingly.

3   **1•18** The next morning you meet a friend, Jamal. You think you recognise his friend Mustafa.

- ◆ Greet him.
- **ahlan fiiki, ya Barbara.**
- ◆ Say hi to his friend, and ask if he is Mustafa.
- **laa', ana mish Mustafa, ismi Mourad!**

quiz

1 When do you say **wa 9alaykum is-salaam**?
2 How do you address a woman formally as *you*?
3 What's the difference between **law samaHt** and **law SamaHti**?
4 Would you use **SabaaH il-khayr** in the morning or the evening?
5 Can you think of three ways of saying *hello*?
6 How do you ask a man his name?
7 What is the correct reply to **tasharrafna**?
8 If tomorrow is **bukra**, how do you say *see you tomorrow* to a male friend?

Now check whether you can ...

- greet someone and respond to their greeting
- ask how they are and tell them how you are
- say good morning, afternoon and evening
- introduce yourself and reply to introductions
- say who you are and ask someone their name
- say goodbye

The best way of developing good Arabic pronunciation is by listening to the audio as often as you can and repeating things out loud, imitating the speakers as closely as you can. It really does make a difference since it familiarises you with the sounds of Arabic and in particular gets you used to those sounds which don't exist in English.

Arabic script: introduction

Arabic is a Semitic language which is read from right to left. It has an alphabet of 28 letters, 14 of which are sun letters and 14 moon letters. Whether a word starts with a sun or moon letter affects the way it sounds when accompanied by **il** *the*. Nouns which start with a moon letter keep the **il** as in: **il-maghrib** *Morocco*, **il-urdun** *Jordan*, whereas nouns which start with a sun letter, replace the **-l** in **il** by that letter: **is-sa9uudiyya** *Saudi Arabia*. This only applies to what is said or read aloud. The **il** always appears in the written form. In MSA (see page 99) *the* is **al** and this is how you'll see it in the script sections. The full alphabet is shown on the next page and, in addition, the letters are introduced in small groups at regular points in the book.

Arabic doesn't use capital letters but some of the letters look different depending on whether they're written on their own or at the beginning, middle or end of a word. Despite the differences, each letter has an essential characteristic which it keeps wherever it occurs.

Arabic letters are intricate, and you'll see that some have similar shapes but vary according to how many dots they have above or below them. Many of the letters join on to each other, most from both right and left. There are many different styles of Arabic script, and Arabic calligraphy is a central feature in Islamic art, with letters and words put together to form superb patterns and shapes.

Reading Arabic script

You don't normally see short vowels (**a**, **i**, **u**) written within words appearing on everyday signs or in newspapers and books, so it's important that you get used to reading without them:

bayt *house* is written **b-y-t** بيت
maktab *office* is written **m-k-t-b** مكتب

The long vowels are represented using the letters, alif ا (**aa**), yaa ي (**ii**) and waw و (**uu**):

maTaar *airport* is written **m-T-aa-r** مطار
mudiir *manager* is written **m-d-ii-r** مدير

There are conventions for representing vowels at the beginning and end of words, which will be introduced as you work through the sections.

When a consonant is doubled in Arabic the letter is only written once. A marker called a 'shadda' ّ can be placed above the letter to show it is doubled, but you won't often see it written in: **jadda** جدّة *Jeddah*.

Isolated letter	Name	Sound	Example		Sun/moon letter
ا	alif	*see below*	باب	baab	☽
ب	baa	b	بيت	bayt	☽
ت	taa	t	تلفون	tilifawn	☀
ث	thaa	th	إثنين	ithnayn	☀
ج	jiim	j	جميل	jamiil	☽
ح	Haa	H	أحمد	aHmad	☽
خ	khaa	kh	أخي	akhi	☽
د	daal	d	مدرسة	madrasa	☀
ذ	dhaal	dh	لذيذ	ladhiidh	☀
ر	raa	r	سيارة	sayyaara	☀
ز	zaa	z	زميل	zamiil	☀
س	siin	s	سوق	suuq	☀
ش	shiin	sh	شمس	shams	☀
ص	Saad	S	مصر	maSr	☀
ض	Daad	D	الرياض	ar-riyaaD	☀
ط	Taa	T	طالب	Taalib	☀
ظ	DHaa	DH	ظُهر	DHuhr	☀
ع	9ayn	9	عندي	9andi	☽
غ	ghayn	gh	غالي	ghaali	☽
ف	faa	f	فندق	funduq	☽
ق	qaaf	q or '	القاهرة	al-qaahira	☽
			مقاس	ma'aas	☽
ك	kaaf	k	كتاب	kitaab	☽
ل	laam	l	لون	lawn	☀
م	miim	m	مدير	mudiir	☽
ن	nuun	n	نور	nuur	☀
ه	haa	h	هو	huwwa	☽
و	waw	w, uu	ولد	walad	☽
ي	yaa	y, ii	يوم	yawm	☽

alif can represent the sound of the long vowel **aa**, and at the beginning of words the short vowels **a**, **i**, **u** (with the hamza, see page 68).

min wayn inta?

talking about where you're from

... and your nationality

saying where you live

giving your phone number

In the Arab world people are always curious to know which country foreign visitors are from and it may be one of the first things you're asked.

The names of most Western countries don't sound very different in Arabic; for example, **hulanda** is *Holland*, **iskutlanda** *Scotland*, **irlanda** *Ireland* and **amriika** *America*.

Certain Arab countries have the word **il** *the* within their name. For example you will hear **maSr** and **lubnaan** for *Egypt* and *Lebanon* but **il-maghrib** and **il-urdun** for *Morocco* and *Jordan*. This is also true for Arabic cities, **baghdaad** is *Baghdad*, **ir-riyaaD** *Riyadh*, and **id-daar il-bayDa** *Casablanca*. **il-jazaa'ir** can mean *Algeria* or *Algiers*.

Talking about where you're from

1   **1•19** Listen to the key language:

min wayn inta/inti?	Where are you from? (to m/f)
ana min briiTaanya.	I'm from Britain.
inta/inti min is-sa9uudiyya?	Are you from Saudi Arabia? (to m/f)
laa', ana min il-maghrib.	No, I'm from Morocco.
ana min il-qaahira kamaan.	I'm from Cairo as well.

---

bil 9arabi ...

the word for *the* is **il**, although the way it appears changes depending on the first letter of the following noun. Of the 28 letters in the Arabic alphabet, 14 are called sun letters and 14 are moon letters. Nouns which start with a moon letter take **il-**: **il-maghrib** *Morocco*. But if a noun starts with a sun letter, the **l** in **il-** is replaced by that letter: **is-sa9uudiyya** *Saudi Arabia*. (Refer to page 16 for the full list of sun and moon letters.)

---

2   **1•20** Farida Haddad is running an Arabic language school in Beirut. She asks her new teachers where they're from. Listen and tick which country each one is from.

	is-sa9uudiyya *Saudi Arabia*	lubnaan *Lebanon*	suuriya *Syria*	maSr *Egypt*	il-urdun *Jordan*
George					
Muhsin					
Tareq					
Nadia					
Ruba					

3   **1•21** Mark Jones is attending a conference in Damascus and asks a fellow delegate which city he comes from. Circle the correct answer:

Taraablus *Tripoli*   **jadda** *Jeddah*   **iskandariyya** *Alexandria*

4   How would you ask Farida where she's from?

... and your nationality

1 **1•22** Listen to the key language:

inta briiTaani?	Are you British? (to m)
inti briiTaaniyya?	Are you British? (to f)
aywa, ana briiTaani/briiTaaniyya.	Yes, I am British. (m/f)
laa', ana mish lubnaani/lubnaaniyya.	No, I'm not Lebanese. (m/f)

---

bil 9arabi ...

you change the ending of the name of a country to get the nationality. The nationality ending for a male is **-i**, while the feminine ending is **-iyya**:

briiTaanya *Britain*	**briiTaani** (m)	**briiTaaniyya** (f) *British*
lubnaan *Lebanon*	**lubnaani** (m)	**lubnaaniyya** (f) *Lebanese*

G7

---

2 **1•23** Match the **jinsiyya** *nationality* to the **balad** *country*, then give the feminine forms. Try saying them out loud, then listen to check.

suuri	**maSri**	**ingliizi**	**iskutlandi**	**maghribi**
sa9uudi	**fransi**	**tuunisi**	**irlandi**	

amriika *America*	**amriiki/amriikiyya**
iskutlanda *Scotland*	
fransa *France*	
ingilterra *England*	
irlanda *Ireland*	
maSr *Egypt*	
il-maghrib *Morocco*	
is-sa9uudiyya *Saudi Arabia*	
tuunis *Tunisia*	
suuriya *Syria*	

---

3 **1•24** The students at Farida's school are getting to know each other. Circle the correct answers to describe their nationalities:

Hussein: **maSri/lubnaani**	Maha: **maghribiyya/lubnaaniyya**
Adam: **irlandi/amriiki**	Jacqueline: **fransiyya/suuriyya**
David: **ingliizi/iskutlandi**	

Saying where you live

1 **1•25** Listen to the key language:

wayn saakin/saakna?	Where do you live? (to m/f)
ana saakin fi dimashq.	I live in Damascus. (m)
ana saakna fi iskandariyya.	I live in Alexandria. (f)
ana mish saakin/saakna fi Halab.	I don't live in Aleppo. (m/f)
inta saakin/inti saakna fil-qaahira?	Do you live in Cairo? (to m/f)

---

bil 9arabi ...

the key word when talking about where you live is saakin. It has three different forms, depending on who's talking or being talked about:

- one male saakin: (ana/inta/huwwa) saakin *I/you/he live(s)*
- one female saakna: (ana/inti/hiyya) saakna *I/you/she live(s)*
- more than one person saakniin

Not is mish: huwwa mish saakin *he doesn't live*

In grammar terms saakin is an active participle, and you'll come across more words that work in the same way. **G12**

---

2 **1•26** Farida asks some of her new Arabic teachers where they live in their home countries. Listen to their conversation and complete the dialogue below.

- **wayn .... fil-urdun, ya Nadia?**
- ◆ **ana saakna .... 9ammaan.**
- **w-inta ya Muhsin, ... saakin?**
- ◆ **ana saakin ...-.........**
- **inta .... fil-qaahira kamaan, ya George?**
- ◆ **laa', ana .... fil-qaahira, ana saakin fi bayruut.**

3 **1•27** At the conference Mark Jones is telling Hasan Shoukry where the other delegates live. Listen and match each person with their city. You'll hear **bass** *but*.

1 Adnan 2 Amira 3 Hussein
4 Mustafa 5 Lucy

Giving your phone number

1   **1•28** Listen to the numbers from 0–10:

0	**Sifr**	4	**arba9a**	8	**tamanya**
1	**waaHid**	5	**khamsa**	9	**tis9a**
2	**itnayn**	6	**sitta**	10	**9ashara**
3	**talaata**	7	**sab9a**		

2   **1•29** Listen and jot down the numbers you hear. ....

3   **1•30** Now listen to these phrases relating to **raqm it-tilifawn** *the telephone number*

shuu raqm tilifawnak/	What's your telephone number?
tilifawnik?	(to m/f)
raqm tilifawn il-bayt ...	My home telephone number (is) ...
raqm il-mubayl ...	The mobile number (is) ...
raqm tilifawn il-maktab ...	The telephone number of the office (is) ...

4   **1•31** Ayman wants to make a note of Hasan's phone numbers at the Cairo conference. See if you can figure out which number is for home, office and mobile. You'll hear **wi** as an alternative to **wa** *and*.

0134 0460 ....   0993 2271 ....   0146 0179 ....

5   **1•32** Farida is on a business trip to London and gives her contact details to a colleague. Try saying her office telephone number before you listen and then make a note of her home and mobile numbers.

raqm tilifawn il-maktab 0144 2776
raqm tilifawn il-bayt ....
raqm il-mubayl ....

---

bil 9arabi ...

when two or more nouns such as *phone number* are used together you only use **il-** *the* on the final noun: **raqm it-tilifawn** *the telephone number* lit. *number the telephone*; **raqm tilifawn il-maktab** *the office telephone number* lit. *number telephone the office*.   **G6**

put it **all together**

1   How would the following people say where they're from and what their nationality is?

Example: Leila - Amman, Jordan
ana min il-urdun, saakna fi 9ammaan. ana urduniyya.

a   Ahmad – Cairo, Egypt
b   Amina – Casablanca, Morocco
c   Zubayr - Jeddah, Saudi Arabia
d   Latifa - Damascus, Syria
e   Ewan – Edinburgh, Scotland

2   Complete the following in words and figures:

a   **tamanya + waaHid** = ...
b   **sitta + itnayn** = ...
c   **sab9a – talaata** = ...
d   **9ashara – khamsa** = ...

3   Lucy Abbot is on business from Newcastle in England. How would she fill in the details in this form?

ism ....

balad ....

jinsiyya ....

4   Can you say these results in Arabic?

Morocco	6	France	2
Tunisia	3	Lebanon	1
Scotland	5	Syria	9
Egypt	4	Jordan	7

1 **1•33** Imagine you are Olivier Jolivet, a Frenchman from Paris studying Arabic in Jordan. You get talking to a waiter in a café.

- **min wayn inta?**
- ◆ Reply, and ask him if he's from Jordan.
- **laa' ana min tuunis. wayn saakin?**
- ◆ Say you live in Paris, and ask his name.
- **ismi Jamal, marHaba.**

2 **1•34** Now take the part of a British woman, Louise Taylor, and answer the waiter's questions.

- **inti min fransa kamaan?**
- ◆ Reply.
- **wayn saakna?**
- ◆ You live in York.
- **shuu ismik?**
- ◆ Reply.

3 **1•35** Jamal would like to invite you for coffee. Listen and write his home number.

Give him your mobile number: 0971 445 376.

quiz

1. If someone tells you **ana min is-sa9uudiyya**, where are they from?
2. Which is the odd one out, and why? **lubnaan**, **maSr**, **maghribi**.
3. How would you tell someone that you're from England and live in London?
4. What are the next two numbers in this sequence: **itnayn**, **arba9a**, **sitta** …, …
5. Would an Egyptian woman say **ana maSriyya** or **ana maSri**?
6. How would you say *He is from Syria*?
7. Would a man or a woman say **ana saakna fi Halab**?
8. How would you ask a business colleague for their office phone number?

Now check whether you can …

- say what your name is
- say where you're from
- say which city you live in
- say what your phone numbers are
- ask others for this information
- use the numbers 0–10

It's a good idea at this stage to start organising your vocabulary learning. Write new words and phrases in a notebook or group them on index cards and review them regularly. Try sticking new words on your mirror or kitchen walls or wherever you'll see them most often. Get friends to test you on vocabulary – they don't need to be Arabic speakers.

Arabic script: 1

The varying forms of the letters are shown as:
- initial: at the beginning of a word or following a letter which only connects from the right
- medial: within a word (i.e. not at the beginning or the end)
- final: at the end of a word
- isolated: used on its own or following a letter which only connects from the right

1   Look at the following six letters. Apart from the **alif** all the others can be joined on both sides to other letters. The **alif** can only be joined from the right and may also appear as أ or إ. See page 68.

Letter	Sound	Isolated	Final	Medial	Initial
alif	aa, a, i, u	ا	ـا	ـا	ا
baa	b	ب	ـب	ـبـ	بـ
taa	t	ت	ـت	ـتـ	تـ
thaa	th	ث	ـث	ـثـ	ثـ
nuun	n	ن	ـن	ـنـ	نـ
yaa	y, ii	ي	ـي	ـيـ	يـ

The **alif** is easy to spot as it is a straight vertical line and you can see that the **yaa** is clearly recognisable because it is the only Arabic letter which has two dots below it. When an **i** appears at the end of a word it is written with the **yaa**.

2   Circle each **alif** you see in the following words:

عمان   سيارة   امس   بريطانيا   البيت   انا

3   Match the following Arabic words with their written form. Do you know what any of them mean?

1 **ana**	5 **baab**	a اثنين	e اب
2 **bint**	6 **banaat**	b ابني	f بنت
3 **ab**	7 **ithnayn**	c انا	g بنات
4 **ibni**		d باب	

Check your answers on page 90.

Arabic script: 2

1   Look at the following letters:

Letter	Sound	Isolated	Final	Medial	Initial
siin	s	س	ﺲ	ﺴ	ﺳ
shiin	sh	ش	ﺶ	ﺸ	ﺷ
kaaf	k	ك	ﻚ	ﻜ	ﻛ
laam	l	ل	ﻞ	ﻠ	ﻟ
miim	m	م	ﻢ	ﻤ	ﻣ

2   Circle the letter **miim** wherever it occurs in the following words:

مكتب   سلام   شمس   محطة   المغرب   أمس

When the letter **laam** is followed by an **alif** as in the word **laa'** *no*, it takes on a special form:

Letter	Sound	Isolated	Final	Medial	Initial
laam alif	laa	لا	ﻼ	ﻼ	لا

3   The word below forms part of a well-known greeting with **laam alif** in the middle. Can you read it?

سلام

4   Match the corresponding words which all start with the letter **miim**. Do you know what any of the words mean?

1 **malik**	a	مكتب
2 **shams**	b	ملك
3 **maktab**	c	شمس
4 **kitaab**	d	كتاب

Check your answers on page 90.

haadi Farida

introducing friends and family

talking about yourself and your family

saying what you do for a living

saying how old you are

In the Arabic-speaking world, family names are used less routinely than in the West. First names are used in most social scenarios. You will also hear people being called by their title, such as **duktuur** *Doctor*. Good friends are often referred to as **akh** *brother* and **ukht** *sister*.

The words **ab** *father* and **umm** *mother* are frequently seen in proper names including place names such as **Abu Dhabi** and **Umm Qasr**. You may hear people use these words to refer to themselves e.g. **abu ahmad** *the father of Ahmad*, **umm Hasan** *the mother of Hasan*.

If a Muslim has been on **Hajj** *pilgrimage* to the Islamic Holy sites of Mecca and Medina, after returning he or she can be referred to as **Hajj** or **Hajja** e.g. **Hajj 9umar** *pilgrim Omar*, **Hajja Maryam** *pilgrim Miriam*.

Introducing friends and family

1   1•36 Listen to the key language:

haada ...	This is ... (m)	**haadi ...**	This is ... (f)
... jawzi.	... my husband.	**... marti.**	... my wife.
... SaaHibi.	... my friend.	**... SaaHibti.**	... my friend.
... zamiili.	... my colleague.	**... zamiilti.**	... my colleague.

2   1•37 Ewan Stewart has been invited to a party at Farida's flat in Beirut. She introduces him to a number of people. Can you figure out who Sinaan and Shahla are?

---

bil 9arabi ...

many nouns referring to people have different masculine and feminine endings, with the feminine usually adding -a:

SaaHib *male friend*   **SaaHiba** *female friend*
zamiil *male colleague*   **zamiila** *female colleague*

To say *my*, the masculine adds -i while the feminine -a is replaced by -ti:

SaaHibi *my male friend*   **SaaHibti** *my female friend*
zamiili *my male colleague*   **zamiilti** *my female colleague*

G1, G5

---

3   1•38 Still at Farida's party, Ewan is introduced to some more people. Listen and complete the dialogue:

Yaser: **haadi .... Layla.**
Ewan: **ahlan wa sahlan.**
Shahla: **ahlan fiik.**
Yaser: **wa haada .... Adnaan.**
Ewan: **marHaba, ya Adnaan!**
Adnaan: **marHabtayn.**
Shahla: **wa .... Marwa.**
Ewan: **tasharrafna.**

Who is Marwa?

4   How would you introduce the following people?
    a your wife, Suzanne   b your husband, John
    c your male colleague, Lutfi   d your female friend, Jamila

Talking about yourself and your family

1   **1•39** Listen to the key language:

inta mitzawwij/inti mitzawwija?	Are you married? (to m/f)
ana mitzawwij/mitzawwija.	I'm married. (m/f)
ana mish mitzawwij/mitzawwija.	I'm not married. (m/f)
9andak/9indik awlaad?	Do you have children? (to m/f)
9andi talaat banaat.	I have three daughters.
9andi ibn waaHid wa bint waaHda.	I have one son and one daughter.
maa 9andi awlaad.	I don't have (any) children.

2   **1•40** Mark Jones, a student of Arabic in Syria, is chatting to two teachers, Nabiil Shukri and Hasna Sabri. Listen to their conversation, decide whether they're married and circle the correct answer.

Nabiil Shukri: married/not married
Hasna Sabri: married/not married
Mark Jones: married/not married

3   **1•40** Now listen again and this time write down how many children they have:

	sons	daughters
Nabiil Shukri		
Hasna Sabri		
Mark Jones		

> **walad/awlaad**
> *child/children or boy/boys*
> **bint/banaat**
> *girl/girls or daughter/daughters*
> **ibn/abnaa'** *son/sons*

---

bil 9arabi ...

there is no verb *to have*. Instead, endings are added onto **9and**. These are the same endings as used to express *my*, *your* etc:

9andi *I have*   **9andak** *you have* (to m)   **9andu** *he has*
                        9andik *you have* (to f)   **9andha** *she has*

To say *I don't have*, you use **maa** rather than **mish**: **maa 9andi** *I don't have*, **maa 9andha** *she doesn't have*.   **G16**

---

4   **1•41** Listen to the conversation at Farida's party between Linda and Samia. Note down what Linda says about herself:

ana ....

Saying what you do for a living

1   1●42 Listen to the key language:

shuu shughlak/shughlik?	What's your job? (to m/f)
ana ...	I'm ...
... mudarris/mudarrisa.	... a teacher. (m/f)
... muHaasib/muHaasiba.	... an accountant. (m/f)
... mumarriD/mumarriDa.	... a nurse. (m/f)
inta Taalib?/inti Taaliba?	Are you a student? (to m/f)
laa', ana mish muhandis/muhandisa.	No, I'm not an engineer. (m/f)
ana Tabiib/Tabiiba fi mustashfa.	I'm a doctor in a hospital. (m/f)

---

bil 9arabi ...

there's no equivalent of *a*, so **Tabiib/Tabiiba** (m/f) mean both *doctor* and *a doctor* and **fi mustashfa** means *in hospital* and *in a hospital*. To say *at school* or *at university* use **fil: ana fil jaami9a** *I'm at university.*   **G9**

---

2   1●43 Listen to some of Farida's students saying what they do and match each person's name to their occupation.

1   2   3 4

a Ewan   **b** Brigitte   **c** John   **d** Hilary

3   1●44 At the conference in Damascus, Mark Jones is briefing a visitor. Listen and note down in English what jobs people do and where.

Ahmad Khaalid ....

Leila Muraad ....

Mahmuud Saber ....

Jumaana Dalaal ....

Salah Nazmi ....

madrasa	*school*
jaami9a	*university*
maktab	*office*
sharika	*company*
ustaaz/ustaaza	*lecturer* (m/f)

4   How would you ask Mark what his job is?

Saying how old you are

1 **1•45** Listen to the numbers from 11–20:

11 **Hida9sh**	16 **sitta9sh**
12 **itna9sh**	17 **sab9ata9sh**
13 **talata9sh**	18 **tamanta9sh**
14 **arba9ta9sh**	19 **tis9ata9sh**
15 **khamasta9sh**	20 **9ishriin**

2 **1•46** Listen and circle the numbers you hear: 11 12 13 14 15 16 17 18 19 20

3 **1•47** Listen to the key language:

9andak/9andik kam sana?	How old are you? (to m/f) *Lit.* You have how many year?
9andi khamasta9shar sana.	I'm fifteen years old. *Lit.* I have fifteen year.
shuu ismu/ismha?	What's his/her name?
kam sana 9andu/9andha?	How old is he/she?
9andu sitta9shar sana.	He is sixteen years old.
9andha sab9a siniin.	She is seven years old.

---

bil 9arabi ...

when using numbers with nouns, 3–10 use the noun in the plural, and drop their final **-a**. Anything over 10 uses the noun in the singular, and numbers 11–19 add **-ar**:
talaat mudarrisiin *three teachers* (m), **itna9sha̲r mudarris** *twelve teachers* (m).

You may have noticed certain nouns change quite dramatically from singular to plural. These have to be learned as you come across them. **G2, G20**

---

4 **1•48** Nabiil Shukri has invited Mark Jones to his house in Damascus and introduces him to his son MuHammed and his friends Hasan and George. Listen and write how old they are.

MuHammed ....   Hasan ....   George ....

5 **1•49** At Farida's party one of the students asks Shahla about her children. Who is older, Latifa or Sinaan?

put it all together

1. Which answer fits best the question?

a	inta mitzawwij, ya Munir?	1	laa', ana mudarrisa.
b	ibnak 9andu kam sana?	2	9andha khams siniin.
c	9andik awlaad, ya Mervat?	3	laa', ana mish mitzawwij.
d	shuu shughlak, ya John?	4	9andu sitta9shar sana.
e	inti Taaliba?	5	ana muHaasib.
f	bintik 9andha kam sana?	6	aywa, 9andi talaat awlaad.

2. This is Ahmad's family tree:

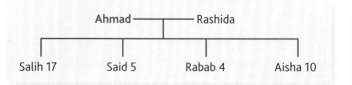

Choose the correct option.

a	Ahmad	• mitzawwij	• mitzawwija
b	Ahmad 9andu	• talaat banaat	• talaat awlaad
c	Rabab 9andha	• arba9 siniin	• arba9ta9shar sana
d	Aisha 9andha	• 9ashar siniin	• khams siniin
e	Salih 9andu	• sitta9shar sana	• sab9ata9shar sana

3. How would Munir introduce these people?

Saida: wife, teacher
Ashraf: friend, married, accountant
Lina: colleague, not married, doctor

1   **1•50** Answer the following questions as if you were David Warren, a teacher from Manchester, married to Rachel, with a daughter Alison, who's 12.

- ● ahlan. min wayn inta?
- ● shuu ismak?
- ● haadi martak?
- ● shuu shuglak?
- ● wa 9andak awlaad?
- ● kam sana 9andha?

2   **1•51** While on a train you get talking to the man sitting next to you who shows you some photos.

- ● Ask if he's married.
- ◆ **aywa**, **ana mitzawwij**.
- ● Point to a picture and ask if that's his wife.
- ◆ **aywa**, **ismha Hiba**.
- ● Ask if he has children
- ◆ **9andi ibn waaHid.**
- ● Ask his name.
- ◆ **ismu Hussein.**
- ● Ask how old Hussein is.
- ◆ **9andu tis9ata9shar sana.**
- ● Ask if Hussein is at school.
- ◆ **laa', huwwa Taalib fi-jaami9at dimashq.**

quiz

1 What is a **mustashfa**?

2 How do you say *one daughter and one son*?

3 What is **9ishriin** minus **arba9ta9shar**?

4 If someone is twenty years old would they use **siniin** or **sana** to give their age?

5 Is **Taaliba** a male or female student?

6 How would you introduce your friend, Rana?

7 If someone says **shuu ismha?** are they talking about a man or a woman?

8 How would a woman say *I'm not married*?

9 **maa 9andi awlaad** means *I don't have children*. So how would you say *I don't have a mobile*?

Now check whether you can ...

- introduce friends and colleagues
- say whether you're married or not
- say if you have children
- talk about your occupation
- ask others for the above information
- use the numbers 11-20
- give your age
- ask how old other people are

A good way to practise talking about your family is to find a **Suura** *photograph* with lots of your family members on it, such as a wedding group. Point to each person and say their name, who they are in relation to you, how old they are. You might be able to say what some of them do for a living, and if there are different nationalities involved you could mention that too.

Arabic script: 3

1   Look at the following new letters, all of which can only be joined from the right.

Letter	Sound	Isolated	Final	Medial	Initial
daal	d	د	ـد	ـد	د
dhaal	dh	ذ	ـذ	ـذ	ذ
raa	r	ر	ـر	ـر	ر
zaa	z	ز	ـز	ـز	ز
waw	w, uu	و	ـو	ـو	و

2   Circle the letter **raa** in the following words. Do you recognise any of them?

عربي   رقم   يسار   سيارة   مدرسة

3   Match the following words:

1 zaar   2 naar   a دور   b نور

3 daar   4 baar   c سور   d ذاب

5 dhaab   6 nuur   e دار   f زار

7 duur   8 suur   g بار   h نار

4   Match the following Arabic first names with the Arabic script:

1 **Zaynab**   a مراد

2 **Anwar**   b زيد

3 **Zayd**   c رمزي

4 **Ramzi**   d زينب

5 **Mourad**   e أنور

5   Can you identify these two Arab countries?

1 السودان   2 سوريا

Check your answers on page 90.

Arabic script: 4

1   Look at the following letters:

Letter	Sound	Isolated	Final	Medial	Initial
jiim	j	ج	ج	ج	ج
Haa	H	ح	ح	ح	ح
khaa	kh	خ	خ	خ	خ
haa	h	ه	ه	ه	ه

2   Put a circle around the letter **haa** each time you see it in the following words:

إسمه   هذا   مهندس   سهل   هذه   هناك

3   Match these signs that you're likely to see at an airport:

1 **jamaarik** *customs*   a جوازات

2 **jawaazaat** *passports*   b دخول

3 **dukhuul** *entrance*   c خروج

4 **khuruuj** *exit*   d جمارك

Many nouns ending in **-a**, for example **madrasa** مدرسة *school*, end with the **ta marbuuTa**. This looks like a **haa** with two dots above it: ة or ة. The **ta marbuuTa** is also used on the end of adjectives to make them feminine: **kibiira** كبيرة *big*, **Saghiira** صغيرة *small*.

4   Read the information about the facilities available at the Safir hotel in Beirut and tick what's available from the list on the right:

1 إنترنيت   a **Hammaam sibaaHa** *swimming pool*

2 حمام سباحة   b **maT9am lubnaani** *Lebanese restaurant*

3 بنك   c **maktab safar** *travel agency*

                      d **bank**

                      e **internet**

Check your answers on page 90.

waaHid 'ahwa, min faDlak

ordering tea and coffee

... and other drinks

offering, accepting, refusing

asking and paying for the bill

Coffee and tea are popular drinks in the Arab World and the café is the traditional meeting place. *Arabic tea* **shaay 9arabi** is often served black *with mint* **bi na9na9** and in a small glass. Coffee in most Arab countries is similar to Turkish coffee and is quite strong, served either **maZbuuT** *semi-sweet* or **sukkar ziyaada** *with extra sugar*. In some of the countries of the Levant, the coffee is spiced **bi Habb il-haal** *with cardamom* and served with **kaas mayya** *a glass of water*.

In hotels and larger cafés, you can also have English tea served with milk and a wide range of Western-style coffees.

When you're invited to an Arab home, you will traditionally be served with either tea or coffee depending on the local custom.

Ordering tea and coffee

1 **1.52** Listen to the key language:

shuu b-tHibb/b-tHibbi?	What would you like? (to m/f)
biddi ...	I'd like ...
... waaHid shaay	... one tea
... wa itnayn 'ahwa.	... and two coffees.
maZbuuT	semi-sweet
bi/biduun sukkar	with/without sugar
bi Haliib aw biduun Haliib?	With milk or without milk?
min faDlak/min faDlik	please (to m/f)
HaaDir.	OK.

---

bil 9arabi ...

when ordering food and drinks, the normal rules of using numbers with nouns are suspended. The convention is to use the countable number with the singular noun, e.g: **itnayn shaay** *two teas*, **talaata shaay** *three teas* etc.

G20

---

2 **1.53** Farida invites some of her students out to a café on the Corniche in Beirut. Listen and make a note of what she orders:

a Number of teas with milk ....

b Number of teas without milk ....

c Number of coffees (semi-sweet) ....

d Number of coffees without sugar ....

3 **1.54** Amal is ordering coffee and tea for herself and her friend Ruba at the Café al-Andalous. Listen and fill the gaps in the dialogue:

● **...... b-tHibbi?**

◆ **min faDlak. biddi waaHid .... wa waaHid ....**

● **......... sukkar aw .... sukkar?**

◆ **shaay biduun sukkar, wa 'ahwa ....**

● **HaaDir.**

... and other drinks

1   **1.55** Listen to the key language:

ayy khidma?	Can I help you? *Lit.* which service
ayy 9aSiir 9andak/9andik?	Which juices do you have? (to m/f)
fiih ...	There is ...
... 9aSiir burtu'aan.	... orange juice.
... 9aSiir lamuun.	... lemon juice.
biddi itnayn 9aSiir manga.	I'd like two mango juices.
9andak/9andik biira?	Do you have beer? (to m/f)
laa', maa fiih biira.	No, there isn't any beer.

2   **1.56** Ewan Stewart is ordering some drinks in a café in Baalbek. Listen and tick from the list below the drinks he orders. What else does Ewan ask the waiter?

9aSiir shammaam *melon juice*	**9aSiir manga**
9aSiir tuffaaH *apple juice*	**9ilbat cola** *can of cola*
'aniinat mayya ma9daniyya	**9aSiir burtu'aan**
a bottle of mineral water	**biira**

3   **1.57** Maha and Samira stop for refreshments. Listen to Maha speaking to the waiter. What does she order? Why doesn't she order apple juice?

---

bil 9arabi ...

the word for *to want* varies from region to region. **biddi** *I want/ would like* is used widely throughout the Levant. It is not a verb and uses the possessive endings (*my/your* etc.):

biddi *I want*   **biddak** *you want* (to m)   **biddik** *you want* (to f)

G16

---

4   How would you order the following from a waitress?

1 tea with milk
2 semi-sweet coffees
1 apple juice
2 melon juices
1 bottle of mineral water
3 beers

Offering, accepting and refusing

1 **1.58** Listen to the key language:

shuu b-tishrab/b-tishrabi?	What would you like to drink? (to m/f) *Lit.* What you drink?
b-tHibb/b-tHibbi shaay aw 'ahwa?	Would you like tea or coffee? (to m/f)
b-aakhud cola bass.	I'll just have a cola. *Lit.* I take cola only
9ashaanak/9ashaanik?	For you? (to m/f)
9ashaani ...	For me ...
laa', shukran.	No thanks.
Tayyib.	Fine. OK.

---

bil 9arabi ...

verbs have both prefixes and endings in the present tense:

	like	*take*	*drink*
I	**aHibb**	**aakhud**	**ashrab**
you (m)	**tiHibb**	**taakhud**	**tishrab**
you (f)	**tiHibbi**	**taakhdi**	**tishrabi**

In the Levant a **b-** prefix is also added before the verb in the present tense. To say you don't do something, you put **maa** first:
maa b-aHibb *I don't like*, **maa b-tishrabi** *you* (f) *don't drink*. **G10**

---

2 **1.59** Nabiil Sha'aban is at a café in Damascus with two friends, Nadia and Hasan. Listen and note what drinks they decide to have.

Nadia .... Hasan ....

3 **1.60** Hasan invites Nabiil for coffee the next day. Number their conversation below in the right order and then listen to check.

biddak 'aniinat mayya kamaan?

9ashaani... b-aakhud 'ahwa bass.

ahlan ya Nabiil! kiif il-haal?

ana b-aakhud 'ahwa bi Haliib, min faDlak.

laa' shukran, maa biddi mayya, w-inta?

bi-khayr shukran. w-inta?

il-Hamdulillaah. shuu b-tishrab?

Asking and paying for the bill

1   **1.61** Listen to the following numbers:

20	**9ishriin**	21	**waaHid wa 9ishriin**
30	**talatiin**	22	**itnayn wa 9ishriin**
40	**arba9iin**	23	**talaata wa 9ishriin**
50	**khamsiin**	24	**arba9a wa 9ishriin**
60	**sittiin**	25	**khamsa wa 9ishriin**
70	**saba9iin**	26	**sitta wa 9ishriin**
80	**tamaniin**	27	**sab9a wa 9ishriin**
90	**tis9iin**	28	**tamanya wa 9ishriin**
100	**miyya**	29	**tis9a wa 9ishriin**

2   **1.62** You're going to hear all but one of the following numbers. Which one is it?

30   65   40   33   20   78   50   22   44

3   **1.63** Say the following numbers out loud, then listen to them to see how you did.

26   53   61   74   77   81   99   100

4   **1.64** Listen to the key language:

il-Hisaab, min faDlak/min faDlik.	The bill, please. (to m/f)
khalli il-baa'i 9ashaanak/9ashaanik.	Keep the change. (to m/f)
shukran kitiir.	Thank you very much.
9afwan.	You're welcome.
itfaDDal/itfaDDali.	Here you are. (to m/f)

5   **1.65** Listen to the waiter telling Hasan Shukri how much his order is and fill in the answers below. Listen out for **il-majmuu9** *the total*.

coffee .... juice .... total ....

6   **1.66** Amal is paying the bill at the Café al-Andalous. Can you figure out how much tip she leaves for the waiter?

put it **all together**

1 Choose a suitable response from the box below

   a **shuu b-tHibb?**

   b **il-Hisaab, min faDlak.**

   c **ayy 9aSiir 9indik?**

   d **fiih biira?**

   e **khalli il-baa'i 9ashaanak.**

   ---
   1 **itfaDDal.**
   2 **fiih 9aSiir manga wa 9aSiir shammaam.**
   3 **shukran.**
   4 **laa', maa fiih.**
   5 **biddi 'aniinat mayya, min faDlak.**

2 Say these numbers in Arabic then write the answers.

   1 26 + 67   2 45 + 33   3 38 + 51

   4 74 – 42   5 81 – 28   6 90 – 66

3 What has been ordered to drink?

   a **b-aakhud waaHid shaay bi sukkar.**

   b **biddi talaata 9aSiir burtu'aan.**

   c **biddi itnayn 'ahwa maZbuuT.**

   d **b-ashrab 9aSiir lamuun.**

   e **9ashaani 'ahwa wa 'aniinat mayya ma9daniyya.**

1   **1.67** You're in a café in Damascus with some friends who don't speak Arabic.

- **ayy khidma?**
- ◆ Order two semi-sweet coffees and one tea.
- **bi Haliib aw biduun Haliib?**
- ◆ Say with milk.
- **HaaDir.**

2   **1.68** You're ready to leave the café.

- Ask the waiter for the bill.
- ◆ **itfaDDali. saba9iin lira.**
- Offer him 80 Syrian pounds, and tell him to keep the change.
- ◆ **shukran kitiir. ma9a as-salaama.**
- ◆ Say goodbye.

3   **1.69** You're at a party in Beirut.

- **ahlan. shuu b-tishrabi?**
- ◆ Say hello to him, and ask if there's any beer.
- **laa', maa fiih biira. 9andi 9aSiir burtu'aan aw 9aSiir tuffaaH.**
- ◆ Say you'll have an orange juice, please.
- **itfaDDali.**

quiz

1 If you say **shukran kitiir**, what will you often hear in reply?
2 How do you say *only*?
3 What is **tamanya wa tamaniin**?
4 Given that **rumaan** is *pomegranate*, how would you ask a waitress *Do you have pomegranate juice?*
5 When ordering a drink from a man, how do you say *please*?
6 Would you use **9ashaani**, **9ashaanak** or **9ashaanik** to order for yourself?
7 How do you ask for something *without sugar*?
8 What is **il-Hisaab**?

Now check whether you can ...

- order tea and different types of coffee
- order cold drinks
- ask someone what they would like to drink
- accept or decline when you're offered a drink
- use the numbers 20–100
- ask for the bill

Teaching another person the Arabic words for various items could help you to remember them better yourself. Enlist the co-operation of a willing friend or member of the family, and when you're out with them, in a pub or a café, teach them how you would place your order for drinks and/or snacks in Arabic.

Checkpoint 1

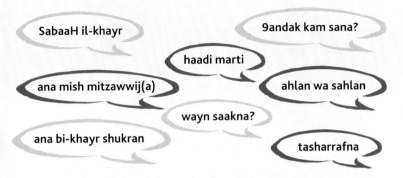

SabaaH il-khayr

9andak kam sana?

haadi marti

ana mish mitzawwij(a)

ahlan wa sahlan

wayn saakna?

ana bi-khayr shukran

tasharrafna

1 Which of the above expressions would you use to ...

  a say hello
  b say you're well, thanks
  c say pleased to meet you
  d ask how old someone is
  e say good morning
  f introduce your wife
  g ask a woman where she lives
  h say that you're not married

2 Identify the odd one out:

a shaay	SabaaH	biira	mayya	'ahwa
b mudarris	muhandis	mumarriD	mubayl	muHaasib
c madrasa	mustashfa	maktab	jaami9a	mitzawwij
d urduni	maSri	sa9uudi	maghribi	tuunisiyya
e akh	ukht	ab	ibn	jawz
f burtu'aan	tuffaaH	manga	9ilba	lamuun
g bint	zamiila	SaaHiba	sharika	mudarrisa
h ahlan	marHaba	masaa il-khayr	is-salaam 9alaykum	Tayyib

3 Look at the information required for the following form. What are the questions you'd need to ask a man to complete it?

Name: ....
Age: ....
Nationality: ....
City of residence: ....
Occupation: ....
Marital status: ....
Children: ....

---

a ....
b ....
c ....
d ....
e ....
f ....
g ....

4 **1•70** Listen to some delegates at a conference in Jordan introducing themselves. Choose the right nationality from the list and complete the table:

---

lubnaani   lubnaaniyya   suuri   suuriyya
ingliizi   ingliiziyya   sa9uudi   sa9uudiyya
maghribi   maghribiyya   maSri   maSriyya

---

il-ism	il-jinsiyya	makaan il-iqaama
name	*nationality*	*place of residence*
Ahmad	....	**il-qaahira**
Lutfi	....	**dimashq**
Naima	....	**ir-ribaaT**
Suhail	....	**ir-riyaaD**
Nadia	....	**bayruut**
Susan	....	**Leeds**

5 **1•71** Listen to the international dialling codes for these countries and add the missing numbers.

1 **liibya** 00 _ _ _   2 **il-maghrib** 00 _ _ _

3 **maSr** 00 _ _ _   4 **il-imaaraat** 00 _ _ _

5 **lubnaan** 00 _ _ _   6 **suuriya** 00 _ _ _

7 **il-urdun** 00 _ _ _   8 **is-sa9uudiyya** 00 _ _ _

6 What questions would you need to ask in order to receive the following answers?

a ....?   fiih 9aSiir manga, wa 9aSiir tuffaaH wa 9aSiir shammaam.

b ....?   biddi itnayn shaay, min faDlik.

c ....?   biduun Haliib.

d ....?   laa', maa fiih 9aSiir lamuun.

e ....?   9ashaani ... b-aakhud 'ahwa bass.

7 **1•72** Practise saying the names of some of the major cities in the Arab world. Listen to check and then match them to their English translations.

1 Halab	2 bayruut	3 il-qaahira	4 ir-riyaaD
	5 9ammaan	6 jadda	7 tuunis
	8 dimashq	9 iskandariyya	10 ir-ribaaT

a Jeddah	b Rabat	c Damascus	d Aleppo
	e Tunis	f Alexandria	g Cairo
	h Amman	i Beirut	j Riyadh

8 **1•73** While waiting at the Abdalleh bus station in Amman you overhear two people talking. Listen then complete their profiles by ticking the correct boxes:

Mona works as a	☐ nurse	☐ doctor
Mona lives in	☐ Rabat	☐ London
Lutfi is	☐ Jordanian	☐ Saudi
Lutfi is	☐ married	☐ single
Mona has a	☐ husband	☐ partner/boyfriend
Lutfi has	☐ no children	☐ one son

9 Look at the drinks menu from Café Salaam and write down in Arabic how much the following items cost.

Café Salaam

shaay	45 L.S.
'ahwa	67 L.S.
9aSiir lamuun	79 L.S.
mayya ma9daniyya	88 L.S.
shaay bi na9na9	55 L.S.
'ahwa bi Haliib	73 L.S.
9aSiir manga	94 L.S.
9aSiir tuffaaH	86 L.S.

---

a mint tea .... **b** lemon juice ....

c mango juice .... **d** apple juice ....

10 Practise ordering some drinks using the phrases learnt in Unit 4. Remember that you can use **biddi** *I'd like*, **b-aakhud** *I'll have*, **9ashaani** *for me*.

a two   **b** one   **c** three   **d** four

e one   **f** two   **g** five   **h** one

law samaHt, fiih maT9am hawn?

asking what there is

... and whereabouts it is

finding out which day places are open

... and what time they're open

Opening times in the Arab World do vary from country to country but as a rule Friday is the weekly day off. In many countries Saturday is also a day off. This will apply to banks and post offices, although foreign exchange facilities are usually open in large hotels every day. North African countries such as Tunisia and Morocco have Sunday as their main day off.

Opening hours are generally 8am-2pm. Some offices open again in the evening. Shops in big cities such as Damascus and Cairo will stay open until 8pm and often later.

There are few **makaatib isti9laamaat** *tourist information offices*. You can ask for local information at hotel receptions, or even hire a taxi for the day with a driver-guide. This is quite common and is good value.

Asking what there is

1 **1•74** Listen to the key language:

mumkin ti'uul/ti'uuli li ...	Can you tell me ... (to m/f)
fiih Saydaliyya hawn?	Is there a chemist's here?
fiih maT9am hawn?	Is there a restaurant here?
laa', maa fiih Saydaliyya hawn.	No, there isn't a chemist's here.
aywa, fiih maTaa9im kitiir.	Yes, there are many restaurants.

2 **1•75** Look at this list of places. Listen and practise saying them:

suu'	**maktab bariid**	**dukkaan**	**dakaakiin**
market	*post office*	*shop*	*shops*

bank	**ba'aal**	**maqha internet**	**matHaf**
bank	*grocer's*	*internet café*	*museum*

suubermarket	**fundu'**	**maHaTTa**	**jaami9**
supermarket	*hotel*	*station*	*Mosque*

3 **1•76** Hiba Mustafa, the receptionist at the Ommayad Hotel in Damascus, tells a group of guests about the district around the hotel. Make a note of the four places she mentions.

1 .... 2 .... 3 .... 4 ....

---

bil 9arabi ...

all nouns in Arabic – not just those referring to people – are either masculine or feminine, e.g. **maT9am** *restaurant* is masculine whereas **Saydaliyya** *chemist's* is feminine.

Most feminine nouns end in **-a**, e.g. **maHaTTa** *station*, although there are some exceptions such as **umm** *mother* and **shams** *sun*. Most nouns not ending in **-a** are masculine e.g. **bayt** *house*. **G1**

---

4 **1•77** Now listen as people ask Hiba questions, and tick or cross the availability of the following.

internet café   supermarket   grocer's   museum

... and whereabouts it is

1   1•78 Listen to the key language:

wayn il-bank biZ-ZabT?	Where is the bank exactly?
il-bank <u>mi'aabil</u> il-fundu'.	The bank is <u>opposite</u> the hotel.
iS-Saydaliyya <u>janb</u> il-mustashfa.	The chemist's is <u>next to</u> the hospital.
maktab il-bariid <u>waraa</u> il-madrasa.	The post office is <u>behind</u> the school.
il-maHaTTa fi <u>wasT</u> il-madiina.	The station is in <u>the centre</u> of town.
is-suu' <u>ba9d</u> maHaTTat il-qiTaar.	The market is <u>past</u> the railway station.

---

bil 9arabi ...

as you saw on page 21, when two nouns are used together you only use **il-** *the* on the second noun: **maktab il-bariid** *the post office* Lit. *office the post*, **wasT il-madiina** *the centre of town* Lit. *centre the town*.

If the first noun normally ends in **-a** then this becomes **-at**: **madrasa** *school*, **madras<u>at</u> il-awlaad** *the boys' school*; **maHaTTa** *station*, **maHaTT<u>at</u> il-qiTaar** *the railway station*.   **G6**

---

2   1•79 Shahla is staying at a hotel in Alexandria and asks the receptionist to point out various places on her map. Listen and work out what A, B, C and D are.

3   1•80 Shahla asks a passer-by where the museum is. Where is it in relation to the station and the bank?

4   1•80 Listen again and note down how she asks where the museum is. ....

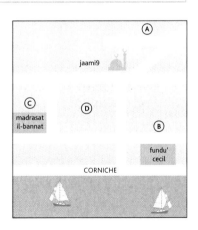

Finding out which day places are open

1 **1•81** Listen to the key language:

il-bank maftuuH aymta?	When is the bank open?
maktab il-bariid maftuuH il-yawm?	Is the post office open today?
huwwa maftuuH/hiyya maftuuHa ...	It is open ... (m/f)
... kull yawm.	... every day.
... <u>min</u> yawm il-aHad <u>li</u> yawm il-khamiis.	... <u>from</u> Sunday <u>to</u> Thursday.
huwwa ma'fuul/hiyya ma'fuula ...	It is closed ... (m/f)

---

bil 9arabi ...

maftuuH/maftuuHa *open* (m/f) and **ma'fuul/ma'fuula** *closed* (m/f)
must agree in gender with what they describe:
il-maT9am maftuuH *the restaurant is open*
iS-Saydaliyya maftuuHa *the chemist's is open*   **G13**

---

2 **1•82** Listen to the days of
the week and practise saying
them.

3 **1•83** Back at the hotel
Shahla asks at reception
when places are open. Tick
the right box.

> **yawm il-aHad** Sunday
> **yawm il-itnayn** Monday
> **yawm it-talaata** Tuesday
> **yawm il-arba9** Wednesday
> **yawm il-khamiis** Thursday
> **yawm il-jum9a** Friday
> **yawm is-sabt** Saturday

	every day	Mon–Sat	Sun–Thurs
is-suubermarket			
iS-Saydaliyya			
maktab il-bariid			

4 **1.83** Listen to the conversation again. Is the post office open today?
What does the receptionist say?

5 **1.84** Mark Jones is at the reception of the Baron Hotel. Listen to the
dialogue and fill in the gaps. You'll hear **bass** *but* and **Hadii'a** *park*.

- **law samaHt, il-matHaf maftuuH .... yawm?**
- **il-matHaf .... il-yawm, bass huwwa .... bukra.**
- **il-Hadii'a .... kull yawm.**

... and what time they're open

1 **1•85** Listen to the key language:

ayy saa9a ...	What time ...
... b-yiftaH/b-tiftaH?	... does it open? (m/f)
... b-yi'fil/b-ti'fil?	... does it close? (m/f)
ayy saa9a b-yiftaH il-matHaf?	What time does the museum open?
b-yiftaH is-saa9a tis9a.	It opens at 9 o'clock. (m)
ayy saa9a b-yi'fil is-suubermarket?	What time does the supermarket close?
b-yi'fil is-saa9a arba9a.	It closes at 4 o'clock. (f)
huwwa maftuuH min is-saa9a tis9a lis-saa9a talaata.	It is open from 9 o'clock to 3 o'clock. (m)

2 **1•86** Practise saying the times below using **is-saa9a** *the time is*.

a   b   c   d   e

---

bil 9arabi ...

verbs agree with, i.e. match, their noun in terms of gender, masculine or feminine:

il-bank b-yiftaH *the bank opens* (m)
il-madrasa b-tiftaH *the school opens* (f)

G10

---

3 **1•87** Listen and note the opening and closing times of these places

		opens	closes
a	museum		
b	restaurant		
c	station		

4 How would you ask what time the market opens?

put it **all together**

1   Match the phrases.

a **is-suu' maftuuH kull yawm.**

1 There isn't an internet café here.

b **ayy saa9a b-yi'fil il-matHaf?**

2 Can you tell me? (to m)

c **il-maHaTTa mi'aabil il-mustashfa.**

3 Where is the post office?

d **il-maktab ma'fuul yawm il-jum9a.**

4 The bank opens at nine o'clock.

e **wayn maktab il-bariid?**

5 What time does the museum close?

f **mumkin ti'uul li?**

6 The station is opposite the hospital.

g **maa fiih maqha internet hawn.**

7 The market is open every day.

h **il-bank b-yiftaH is-saa9a tis9a.**

8 The office is closed on Fridays.

2   Read the information below, and practise telling an Arabic-speaking visitor about the opening and closing times shown as in the following example:

bank: Mon–Fri, 9:00–4:00.
il-bank maftuuH min yawm il-itnayn li yawm il-jum9a.
b-yiftaH is-saa9a tis9a. b-yi'fil is-saa9a arba9a.

a   museum: Tues–Thurs, 9:00–5:00.

b   chemist's: every day, 8:00–7:00.

c   grocer's: Mon–Sat, 10:00–6:00.

3   Describe what there is in your town. Starting with **fi madiinti** in my town. Remember to use **fiih ...** there is/there are ..., and **kitiir** many.

1   **1•88** You're visiting Aleppo and you ask a man at a kiosk for some information.

- Say *excuse me* and ask if there's an internet café in the area.
- **aywa, fiih maqha internet mi'aabil il-bank.**
- Now ask where the **9alaa' id-diin** *Aladdin* restaurant is.
- **il-maT9am janb is-suu'.**
- Thank him and say goodbye.
- **allaah yisalmak.**

2   **1•89** Back at the Baron Hotel in Aleppo you ask Rachida the receptionist about opening times.

- Say *excuse me* and ask what time the post office opens.
- **maktab il-bariid b-yiftaH is-saa9a tamanya.**
- Now ask if it's open every day.
- **laa', huwwa ma'fuul yawm il-aHad.**
- Ask if the museum is open today.
- **laa', huwwa ma'fuul il-yawm. il-matHaf maftuuH bukra.**
- Thank her.
- **ahlan wa sahlan.**

quiz

1 What comes next: **yawm il-arba9, yawm il-khamiis ...** ?

2 How do you say *when* and *where* in Arabic?

3 What are the opposites of these words: **fiih, ma'fuul, b-yiftaH**?

4 What is the plural of **dukkaan**?

5 If someone says **il-bank mi'aabil il-maHaTTa**, is it *next to* or *opposite* the station?

6 Which is the odd one out: **Saydaliyya, fundu', waraa?** What does it mean?

7 Which would you expect to be open **kull yawm: il-matHaf** or **il-mustashfa**?

8 Given **maHaTTat il-qiTaar** means *the railway station* lit. *station of the railway*, how would you say *the hotel restaurant*?

Now check whether you can ...

- approach someone politely
- understand and say the words for places in a town
- ask if there's a particular place nearby
- understand basic phrases as to where a place is
- ask when a place is open
- recognise days of the week
- understand basic times

To help you remember the Arabic you learn, bring it into your everyday life as much as you can. Practise saying what there is and isn't in your home town. You could also imagine you're telling an Arabic-speaking visitor when places are open where you live, for example, banks, supermarkets, shops.

Arabic script: 5

1 Look at the following four letters:

Letter	Sound	Isolated	Final	Medial	Initial
Saad	S	ص	ص	ـصـ	صـ
Daad	D	ض	ض	ـضـ	ضـ
Taa	T	ط	ط	ـطـ	ط
DHaa	DH	ظ	ظ	ـظـ	ظـ

2 Circle the letter **Taa** each time you see it in the following words. Do you recognise any of them?

فطور   قطار   مطعم   طلب   مطار

3 If you see this sign on a motorway approaching **al-maTaar ad-dawli** *the international airport*, which one of the United Arab Emirates are you in?

مطار أبو ظبي الدولي ✈

4 You are at Marrakesh station looking at the **al-wuSuul** الوصول *arrivals* and **adh-dhahaab** الذهاب *departures* board.

al-wuSuul	الوصول	adh-dhahaab	الذهاب
09.30	طنجا	09.20	الجديدة
10.00	الرباط	09.35	الدار البيضاء
11.05	المطار	10.40	طنجا

1 What time does the train for Tangiers (**Tanja**) leave?
2 Has the 10.00 train arrived from Rabat (**ar-ribaaT**) or El Jadida (**al-jadiida**)?
3 Is the Casablanca (**ad-daar al-bayDaa'**) train departing or arriving?
4 Is there a train to the airport between 09.30 and 11.00?

Check your answers on page 90.

Arabic script: 6

1 Look at the following two letters:

Letter	Sound	Isolated	Final	Medial	Initial
9ayn	9	ع	ع	ﻌ	ﻋ
ghayn	gh	غ	ﻎ	ﻐ	ﻏ

2 Circle the letter **9ayn** wherever it occurs in the following words:

مطعم نعم عمل مصنع شارع عندي

3 You want to order a mint tea (**shaay bi na9na9**) and a grape juice (**9aSiir 9inab**). Can you find them on the menu opposite?

a
b
c
d

alif maqSuura appears at the end of certain words and is pronounced **a**. It looks like a **yaa** without the two dots (ى or ﯨ) as in: **mustashfa** مستشفى *hospital*.

alif tanwiin is an **alif** with two small lines above it أ and is pronounced **an** as in **shukran** شكراً *thank you*.

4 Match the following Arabic words ending with **alif maqSuura**:

1 **mabna** *building* 2 **maqha** *cafe* 3 **9ala** *on* 4 **ila** *towards*

a مقهى b إلى c مبنى d على

5 Your hotel in Beirut is on **shaari9 al-maghrib** *Morocco Street*. Tick the correct street name from the list of streets below:

1 شارع لبنان 2 شارع عبد العزيز
3 شارع المغرب 4 شارع الحمراء

Check your answers on page 90.

kiif aruuH lis-suu'?

asking the way

... and following directions

making enquiries

... and getting help to understand

The majority of Arab towns and cities have mediaeval Islamic 'cores' with very narrow streets and alleyways often surrounded by ancient walls. Some of the largest of these cities are **marraaksh** *Marrakesh* and **faas** *Fez* in Morocco, **dimashq** *Damascus* and **Halab** *Aleppo* in Syria, and **il-qaahira** *Cairo* in Egypt. Attached to the old cities where the famous **aswaa'** *souks/markets* are located are the more modern sections which were developed during the Ottoman, French or British colonial periods. Cities in countries under French rule often have areas modelled on the Parisian-style layout.

The Arab world also has great port cities such as **id-daar il-bayDa** *Casablanca*, **il-azaa'ir** *Algiers*, **iskandariyya** *Alexandria*, **bayruut** *Beirut* and **jadda** *Jeddah*.

Asking the way

1   **2•1** Listen to the key language:

wayn a'rab suubermarket?	Where is the nearest supermarket?
kiif aruuH lis-suu'?	How do I get to the market? *Lit.* How do I go to the market?
huwwa/hiyya ...	It's ... (m/f)
... 9ala Tuul.	... straight ahead.
... fi aakhir ish-shaari9.	... at the end of the road.
... fi awwal shaari9 9al-yasaar.	... on the first street on the left.
... fi taani shaari9 9al-yamiin.	... on the second street on the right.
aasif/asfa. maa b-a9raf.	I'm sorry. I don't know. (m/f)

2   **2•2** Whilst on a visit to Amman, Sarah Walker asks where the market is. Listen and pick out from the above list the two pieces of information she's given.

     a ....   b ....

---

bil 9arabi ...

ordinal numbers i.e. *first*, *second* etc., which are adjectives, can come before or after the noun. When they come before the noun they use the masculine form: **awwal shaari9** *(the) first street*, **taani shaari9** *(the) second street*.

When they come after the noun they have to agree with the noun in gender, and both the ordinal number and the noun take **il-** *the*: **ish-shaari9 it-taani** *the second street* Lit. *the street the second*, **taani madrasa** *second school*, **il-madrasa it-taanya** *the second school* Lit. *the school the second*.   **G7**

---

3   **2•3** Listen as Mark Jones asks for directions, then answer the questions below.

- Where does Mark want to go? ● What does the first person say?
- What directions is he given?

4   **2•4** How would you ask a female passer-by how you get to the bank? Now listen as she gives you some information and note its exact location.

... and following directions

1 **2•5** Listen to the key language:

ruuH/ruuHi li ishaarat il-muruur.	Go as far as the traffic lights. (to m/f)
ruuH/ruuHi 9ala Tuul.	Go straight on. (to m/f)
liff/liffi yamiin.	Turn right. (to m/f)
khud/khudi ...	Take ... (to m/f)
... awwal yasaar.	... the first left.
... taani yamiin.	... the second right.

2 **2•6** Sarah is being given directions to the bank, museum and market. Listen and label the boxes marked 1 to 3 on the map. You'll hear **ba9dayn** *then, afterwards.*

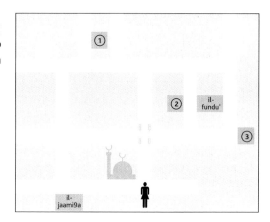

---

bil 9arabi ...

instructions, e.g. *Go, Take, Turn* are created from the present tense of the verb without its prefixes:

b-aruuH *I go*, **ruuH/ruuHi** *Go* (to m/f)
b-aliff *I turn*, **liff/liffi** *Turn* (to m/f)
b-aakhud *I take*, **khud khudi** *Take* (to m/f)

Sometimes an i or u is placed on the front to help with pronunciation: **b-aftaH** *I open*, **iftaH/iftaHi** *Open* (to m/f). **G14**

---

3 **2•7** Look at the map again and listen to the directions Sarah is given from the hotel to the university. Which person gives the correct directions?

Making enquiries

1 **2•8** Listen to some numbers between 100 and 2,000:

101	**miyya wa waaHid**	500	**khamasmiyya**
102	**miyya wa itnayn**	600	**sittmiyya**
120	**miyya wa 9ishriin**	700	**sab9amiyya**
150	**miyya wa khamsiin**	800	**tamanmiyya**
200	**miitayn**	900	**tis9amiyya**
300	**talatmiyya**	1,000	**alf**
400	**arba9miyya**	2,000	**alfayn**

miyya changes to **mitt** before a noun

2 **2•9** Try saying these numbers then listen to check:
130   250   580   634   771   999

3 **2•10** Listen to the key language:

huwwa 'ariib/hiyya 'ariiba?	Is it near? (m/f)
huwwa ba9iid/hiyya ba9iida?	Is it far? (m/f)
<u>**Hawaali**</u> **... min hawn.**	It's <u>about</u> ... from here.
... khamasmiit mitr	... 500m
... 9ishriin da'ii'a	... 20 minutes
mumkin taakhudni li ...	Can you take me to ... (to m)

4 **2•11** Listen as David Warren takes a taxi to his hotel in the Hamra district of Beirut. You'll hear **ta'riiban** as an alternative to **Hawaali**.

a What does the taxi driver say about the Cedarland Hotel?

b How long does he say it will take to get there?

c How far down **9abd il-9aziiz** *Abdel Aziz* street is the hotel?

---

bil 9arabi ...

the words for *near* and *far* are **'ariib** and **ba9iid**. They are adjectives so have to agree in gender with what they describe.
il-maktab 'ariib? *Is the office near?*; **laa', il-jaami9a mish 'ariiba.**
No, the university isn't near.   **G7**

---

5 **2•12** David is looking for an internet café. How far away is it?

6 How would you ask the following in Arabic?
a Is the market near here?   **b** Can you take me to the university?

... and getting help to understand

1   **2•13** Listen to the key language:

mumkin marra taanya?	Can you repeat that? *Lit.* possible second time
mumkin titkallam/ titkallami shway, shway?	Can you speak slowly? (to m/f)
b-titkallam/b-titkallami ingliizi?	Do you speak English? (to m/f)
b-atkallam ingliizi shwayya.	I speak a little English.
maa b-atkallam 9arabi.	I don't speak Arabic.
mish faahim/faahma.	I don't understand. (m/f)

2   **2•14** In Aleppo Ewan Stewart isn't sure how to get to the **maHaTTat il-qiTaar** *railway station*.

    a   Tick any of the key phrases above that you hear him say.
    b   Where is the railway station?

3   **2•15** While visiting the Roman ruins at Jerash, a Jordanian tries to strike up a conversation with Sarah. Listen and number the dialogue in the order you hear it.

ahlan, ana ismi Abdallah.

HaDirtak b-titkallam ingliizi?

min wayn HaDirtik?

aah, ana faahma! ana min amriika. ismi Sarah.

ahlan. min wayn HaDirtik?

ahlan fiik. b-atkallam 9arabi shwayya.

laa', b-atkallam 9arabi bass. ana min il-urdun. min wayn inti?

mumkin titkallam shway shway, law samaHt?

---

bil 9arabi ...

to make a request you can add **mumkin** *possible, can* in front of a verb without the **b-** prefix: **b-aruuH** *I go*; **mumkin aruuH.** *I can go./Can I go?*; **b-titkallam** *you speak*; **mumkin titkallam/ titkallami.** *You can speak./Can you speak?* (to m/f)   **G17**

put it all together

1 Match the Arabic with the English.

a	**mumkin marra taanya, min faDlak?**	1	Can you speak slowly please? (to m)
b	**mumkin titkallam shway shway, law samaHt?**	2	I speak a little Arabic.
c	**b-atkallam 9arabi shwayya.**	3	Do you speak English? (to f)
d	**maa b-atkallam ingliizi.**	4	I don't understand. (f)
e	**mish faahma.**	5	Could you repeat that, please? (to m)
f	**HaDirtik b-titkallami ingliizi?**	6	I don't speak English.

2 Fill in the gaps with the words in the box.

khamasmiit   taani   a'rab   aakhir   'ariib   taakhudni   ti'uul li

a **mumkin .... wayn is-suu'?**
b **law samaHt, wayn .... Saydaliyya?**
c **fiih fundu' fi .... ish-shaari9.**
d **fiih maT9am .... min hawn?**
e **maktab il-bariid fi .... shaari9 9al-yasaar.**
f **mumkin .... lil-jaami9, law samaHt?**
g **ta'riiban .... mitr min hawn.**

3 Rearrange the following into a conversation:

a **mumkin marra taanya, min faDlak?**
b **ruuHi 9ala Tuul, ba9dayn khudi awwal shaari9 9al-yamiin.**
c **shukran.**
d **laa', mish ba9iid. Hawaali arba9miit mitr min hawn.**
e **law samaHt, kiif aruuH lil-matHaf?**
f **ruuHi 9ala Tuul, ba9dayn khudi awwal shaari9 9al-yamiin.**
g **huwwa ba9iid?**

Where does she want to go? What directions is she given? How far away is it?

1 **2•16** You are in the centre of Damascus and need some directions.

- Say excuse me to a passer-by and ask him where the nearest bank is.
◆ **ta'riiban miitayn mitr min hawn 9al-yasaar.**
- You missed that. Ask him to repeat it.
◆ **ta'riiban miitayn mitr min hawn 9al-yasaar.**
- Thank him, then say goodbye.
◆ **allaah yisalmak.**

2 **2•17** Take the part of Laura Smith, who is lost.

- Stop a passer-by and ask her if she speaks English.
◆ **laa', maa b-atkallam ingliizi.**
- Ask her how to get to the railway station from here.
◆ **ruuHi 9ala Tuul, ba9dayn khudi taani shaari9 9al-yamiin. wa maHaTTat il-qiTaar fi aakhir ish-shaari9.**
- Say sorry, you don't understand.
◆ **ruuHi 9ala Tuul, ba9dayn khudi taani shaari9 9al-yamiin.**
- Repeat the information you've been given, then ask if it's far.
◆ **shwayya, mish ba9iida kitiir – ta'riiban kilomitr waaHid min hawn.**
- Thank her.
◆ **9afwan.**

quiz

1 Would you turn right or left if someone told you **liff yamiin**?
2 What's the opposite of **'ariib**?
3 Which one of these is not an instruction? **liff**, **khudi**, **aruuH**.
4 Which is further **khamasmiit mitr** or **talatmiit mitr**?
5 How would you ask a man to repeat something?
6 What does **shway**, **shway** mean?
7 How would a woman say *I'm sorry, I don't know*.
8 What do you think **maa b-atkallam fransi** means?

Now check whether you can ...

- ask where a place is and how to get there
- follow some basic directions
- understand distances
- ask someone to repeat what they've said and to speak more slowly
- check if someone speaks English
- say you speak a little Arabic
- say you don't know or understand
- count to 2,000

Practise what you've learnt in this unit by using **wayn** and **kiif aruuH** to ask where the places are you learnt in Unit 5, and how you'd get to them. Then have a go at counting in Arabic without looking at the book.

Arabic script: 7

1 Look at the following two letters:

Letter	Sound	Isolated	Final	Medial	Initial
faa	f	ف	ـف	ـفـ	فـ
qaaf	q or '	ق	ـق	ـقـ	قـ

2 Match the following foods which all contain the letter **faa**:

1 fuul   **2 kunaafa**   **3 falaafil**   **4 kufta**   **5 filfil** *pepper*

a كنافة   b فلفل   c كفتة   d فلافل   e فول

The **qaaf** is pronounced as a **q** in MSA but in Egypt and parts of the Levant it is pronounced as a glottal stop in everyday words such as:
'ahwa قهوة *coffee*; **'amiiS** قميص *shirt*.

You will hear the **qaaf** pronounced as a **q** even in spoken Egyptian and Levantine Arabic in more sophisticated words such as:
al-qaahira القاهرة *Cairo*; **al-qur'aan** القرآن *The Qur'an*.

Written Arabic	Spoken Levant and Egypt	MSA	Meaning
قهوة	'ahwa	qahwa	*coffee*
قميص	'amiiS	qamiiS	*shirt*
أزرق	azra'	azraq	*blue*

3 Do you know what these signs mean? Where might you see them?

1 مقفول   2 مفتوح

4 Match the following words:

1 **maHaTTa**   5 **suuq**
2 **funduq**   6 **ghurfa**
3 **maSr**   7 **matHaf**
4 **baqqaal**

a متحف   e غرفة
b بقال   f محطة
c فندق   g مصر
d سوق

Check your answers on page 90.

Arabic script: the hamza

The **hamza** is a letter which looks like a small hat ء. It has the sound of a silent cough or a glottal stop similar to the Cockney wa'er (water). There are rules for how it is used depending on where it appears in a word:

- At the beginning of a word the **hamza** always appears on or below an **alif**, and is known as **alif hamza**.
  If the initial **hamza** is followed by **a** or **u** then it sits on the **alif** أ.
  If the initial **hamza** is followed by **i** then it sits below the **alif** إ.
  In colloquial Arabic you rarely see the **hamza** represented in the transliteration.

1 Match the following words which begin with **alif hamza**:

1 **ana**   2 **ismi**   3 **ukhti**   4 **abi**   5 **ummi**   6 **akhi**

a أختي   b أمي   c أنا   d أخي   e أبي   f إسمي

- In certain circumstances the **hamza** is omitted from the beginning of a word altogether. The most common example is when the definite article **al-** ال *the* is used. You will notice this on signs:
  al-qaahira القاهرة *Cairo*; **al-wuSuul** الوصول *arrivals*

- At the end of a word the **hamza** sometimes sits on its own on the line. This can be clearly seen in the feminine form of colours:
  sayyaara Hamraa' سيارة حمراء *a red car*

2 Match the following feminine colours, all of which end with the **hamza** sitting on its own on the line:

1 **bayDaa'** ◯   4 **Safraa'** ◯   a سوداء   d زرقاء

2 **sawdaa'** ●   5 **zarqaa'** ◉   b خضراء   e بيضاء

3 **khaDraa'** ◔   c صفراء

3 Can you recognise this famous Arab city which ends with a **hamza**?

الدار البيضاء

Check your answers on page 90.

'addaysh haada?

asking for what you want

understanding the price

shopping in a market

bargaining

There are many different currencies throughout the Arab world, the main ones being: **dirham**: Morocco and UAE; **gineeh** *pound:* Egypt and Sudan; **lira** *pound*: Syria and Lebanon; **dinaar**: Algeria, Bahrain, Kuwait, Tunisia, Libya, Jordan and Iraq; **riyaal**: Saudi Arabia, Qatar and Oman. The *British pound* is referred to as **gineeh isterliini** as opposed to **gineeh maSri** for the *Egyptian pound*.

Prices are normally fixed in shops, but bargaining is the custom in the **suu'** regardless of whether the customer is Arab or non-Arab. Bargaining is part of the culture and can be very enjoyable and usually both customer and seller are happy with the end result.

The symbol for the Egyptian pound is £E. The various symbols for **lira suuriyya** *Syrian pound* are £S, S£, SP, and L.S.

Asking for what you want

1   2•18 Listen to the key language:

mumkin ashuuf …	Can I have a look at …
… haada-l 'amiiS.	… this/that shirt (m).
… haadi-sh shanTa.	… this/that bag (f).
… ma'aas <u>akbar</u>?	… a <u>larger</u> size?
mumkin a'iisu/a'iisha?	Can I try it on? (m/f)
kibiir/kibiira (shwayya).	It's (too) big. (m/f)
Saghiir/Saghiira (shwayya).	It's (too) small. (m/f)

---

bil 9arabi …

adjectives follow nouns and agree with them in gender and use of
the definite article: **'amiiS kibiir** *a big shirt* (m); **il-'amiiS il-kibiir**
the big shirt. Lit. *the shirt the big*. For most colours the feminine is
formed by removing the a- from the beginning of the masculine
and placing it at the end: **akhDar/khaDra** *green* (m/f); **'amiiS**
akhDar *a green shirt*; **ish-shanTa il-khaDra** *the green bag*.   **G7**

---

2   2•19 Linda wants to buy an **isharb** *scarf* from the Hamidiyyeh Market
in Damascus. You'll hear **alwaan taanya** meaning *other colours*.

aHmar/Hamra	■	akhDar/khaDra	▨	azra'/zar'a	■
aswad/sawda	■	aSfar/Safra	▨	abyaD/bayDa	☐

Listen to the conversation and circle the colours you hear mentioned.

3   2•20 Ewan Stewart sees a shirt he likes in a Beirut shop window.
Listen and decide which statements are TRUE or FALSE:
a   he wants a blue shirt
b   the shirt is too small
c   there isn't a large size

4   2•21 Amal Ayyoubi is in Marrakesh and wants to buy a handbag.
Listen to the dialogue and complete the extracts below.
Which **lawn** *colour* does Amal think is **Hilu/Hilwa**
pretty (m/f)?

- **mumkin ashuuf haadi-sh shanTa** ……………?
- ◆ **b-tHibbi haadi-sh shanTa** …………..?
- **laa', maa b-aHibb il-lawn** ………………
- ◆ **shuufi haadi-sh shanTa** ………………

il-aHmar
il-Hamra
il-khaDra
iz-zar'a

Understanding the price

1   2•22 Listen to the key language:

'addaysh ...	How much is/are ...
... hadawl?	... these/those?
... hadawl il-kuruut?	... these postcards?
hadawl bi miyya wa saba9iin dinar.	Those are 170 dinars.
haada ghaali/haadi ghaalya (kitiir).	It's (very) expensive. (m/f)
9andak/9andik shi <u>arkhaS</u>?	Do you have anything <u>cheaper</u>? (to m/f)

---

bil 9arabi ...

to make comparisons first remove the vowels from the adjective. With **kibiir** *big* this leaves you the root letters **k b r**, to which you add **a** at the beginning and after the second root letter: **akbar** *bigger/biggest*. There's no separate feminine form: **Saghiir** *small*, **aSghar** *smaller/smallest*; **rakhiiS** *cheap*, **arkhaS** *cheaper/cheapest*.

The comparative, e.g. *bigger* comes after the noun: **ma'aas akbar** *a bigger size*. The superlative e.g. *biggest* comes before the noun, as in English, but it does not require the definite article *the*: **akbar ma'aas** *the biggest size*.   **G21**

---

2   2•23 Farida is on a trip to Amman and is asking the prices of various items in a clothes shop. Listen and write in the prices for the following:

a **bluuza**   b **fustaan**   c **jakayt**

3   Why is the dress so expensive?

4   2•24 Mark Jones wants to buy a few things from the **kushk** *kiosk* next to his hotel. Listen and note which items match the prices below:

a £E20 ....   b £E80 ....   c £E90 ....   d £E200 ....

---

jariida/jaraa'id *newspaper(s)* **majalla/majallaat** *magazine(s)* **kitaab/ kutub** *book(s)* **Taabi9/Tawaabi9** *stamp(s)* **kart/kuruut** *postcard(s)*

Which item is not available? Where is he told to go?

5   How would you say:
   ● This bag is very expensive.   ● How much are these books?

Shopping in a market

1   2•25 Listen to the key language:

mumkin ashuufu?	Can I see it? (m)
mumkin ashuufha?	Can I see it (f)/them?
'addaysh biddak/biddik?	How many do you want? (to m/f)
b-aakhud …	I'll have *Lit*. I take …
… haada/haadi.	… this one. (m/f)
… hadawl/khamsa min hadawl.	… these/five of these.
b-aakhdu.	I'll take it. (m)
b-aakhudha.	I'll take it (f)/them.
biddak/biddik shi taani?	Would you like anything else? (to m/f)

2   2•26 Linda is visiting Aleppo's famous covered market. You'll hear a shopkeeper telling her what she might find. Tick the items you hear. Listen out for **laakin** *but* and **mumtaaz/mumtaaza** *excellent* (m/f).

tawaabil *spices*	**SaHn/SuHuun** *large dish(es)*
finjaan/fanaajiin *cup(s)*	**ibrii' shaay** *tea pot*
Siniyya/Sawaani *tray(s)*	**ibrii' 'ahwa** *coffee pot*

3   2•27 Linda is at another stall and asks about two items. Which ones does she ask for? What does she buy? Listen out for **bass** which in this context means *only*.

4   2•28 In Damascus Mark Jones wants to buy some traditional **fukhaar** *earthenware* in the Hamidiyyeh Market. Listen and write in the quantity of each item he asks for:

cups …………………… dishes …………………… coffee pots ……………………

---

bil 9arabi …

because nouns are either masculine or feminine, you use *him* and *her* for the English *it*. *Him* is translated by adding **-u** to the verb, *her* by adding **-ha**:

b-aakhdu *I'll take it* (m); **b-aakhudha** *I'll take it* (f)
a'iisu *I try it on* (m); **a'iisha** *I try it on* (f)

-ha is also used for *them* when referring to inanimate objects of either gender: **b-aakhudha** *I'll take them*.

Bargaining

1   **2•29** Listen to the key language:

biddi ashuuf bass.	I'm just looking. *Lit.* I want I look only.
biddi ashtiri …	I want to buy …
shuu aHsan taman 9andak/9andik?	What's your best price? (to m/f)
miitayn lira mniiH?	Is 200 Syrian pounds OK?
mish mumkin.	It's not possible.

2   **2•30** Sarah Walker joins Mark at the market and sees a coffee pot she likes. Listen and make a note of:

a the original price in Syrian pounds ....
b how much she agrees on after some hard bargaining ....

3   **2•30** Listen again. Did you hear how the shopkeeper agreed to Sarah's final price?

Note it down in English and Arabic. ....

---

bil 9arabi …

there is no infinitive e.g. *to buy*, *to drink*. You literally say *I want I buy*, *you want you buy* etc: **biddi ashtiri** *I want to buy* Lit. *I want I buy*; **biddak tishtiri** *you want to buy* Lit. *you want you buy*.

---

4   **2•31** Mark continues his stroll around the market and a vendor attracts his attention. Listen to the dialogue and fill in the gaps with the words in the box:

- **itfaDDal, itfaDDal ya akhi. shuu biddak ....?**
- **biddi .... bass.**
- **haada-S SaHn jamiil kitiir.**
- **laa', shukran maa biddi ....**
- **iS-Siniyya bi miitayn lira bass!**
- **miyya wa khamsiin lira ....?**
- **laa', mish mumkin.**
- **shuu .... taman 9andak?**
- **miyya wa saba9iin lira.**
- **................**

> **jamiil/jamiila**
> *beautiful* (m/f)

mniiH	**ashtiri**	**b-aakhudha**
ashuuf	**tishtiri**	**aHsan**

put it all together

1   Which is the odd one out? Why?

   a **bluuza, 'amiiS, isharb, Siniyya**

   b **rakhiiS, akbar, aSghar, aghla**

   c **dinaar, gineeh, dirham, miyya**

   d **abyaD, aswad, akbar, azra'**

2   Fill in the gaps with the words in the box.

> **arkhaS**   **il-aswad**   **akbar**   **mumtaaz**
>
>   **il-Hilwa**   **iz-zar'a**   **kibiir**   **il-aHmar**

   a **'addaysh ish-shanTa _____?** (*blue*)

   b **b-aakhud haada-l isharb _____** (*black*)

   c **biddi ashtiri il-bluuza _____** (*pretty*)

   d **il-jakayt _____ kitiir.** (*big*)

   e **mumkin a'iis il-fustaan _____?** (*red*)

   f **mumkin ashuuf _____ ibrii' 'ahwa 9andak?** (*biggest*)

   g **9andik 'amiiS _____?** (*cheaper*)

   h **haada-l kitaab _____** (*excellent*)

3   Choose the correct option for each sentence from the pair given below.

   a **b-aHibb iS-SaHn. mumkin _____?**

   b **biddi _____ khamsa min hadawl.**

   c **haadi-S Siniyya Hilwa kitiir. _____.**

   d **9andik _____ fustaan lawn akhDar?**

   e **it-tawaabil mumtaaza. _____**

   f **'addaysh _____ fanaajiin?**

> a **ashuufu/ashuufa**   b **ashtiri/tishtiri**
>
> c **b-aakhdu/b-aakhudha**   d **haadi-l/haada-l**
>
> e **b-aakhdu/b-aakhudha**   f **haada-l/hadawl il-**

now you're talking!

1 **2•32** Imagine you're visiting Aleppo and doing a bit of shopping in the **suu'**.

- **ahlan. SabaaH il-khayr.**
- ◆ Reply, and ask how much the white shirt is.
- **il-'amiiS bi miyya wa 9ishriin lira.**
- ◆ Ask if you can try it on.
- **itfaDDal.**
- ◆ Say it's a bit small. Ask if he has a larger size.
- **laa', maa 9andi.**

2 **2•33** Now you're looking for a leather handbag for your sister. You'll hear **itfaDDal** meaning *come this way*.

- **marHaba, ahlan wa sahlan. itfaDDal.**
- ◆ Say excuse me, and ask the woman how much this handbag is.
- **haadi bi tis9amiit lira suuriyya.**
- ◆ Ask if she has the bag in red.
- **9andi bass aswad wa azra'.**
- ◆ Say OK, you'll take the blue bag.

3 **2•34** Now for some souvenirs. You'll hear **kwayyis** *good*.

- **aywa? ayy khidma?**
- ◆ Ask if you could have a look at this tray.
- **itfaDDal**.
- ◆ Ask how much it is.
- **haadi bi miitayn lira.**
- ◆ Say that it's very expensive. Ask if 120 is ok.
- **laa' mish mumkin.**
- ◆ Ask what his best price is.
- **miyya wa sittiin kwayyis?**
- ◆ Offer 150 Syrian pounds.
- **Tayyib, itfaDDal.**

quiz

1 What's the difference between **iS-SaHn jamiil** and **iS-SaHn il-jamiil**?

2 Which is more: **miitayn riyaal** or **itnayn riyaal**?

3 Change the word **Tawiil** *tall* to *taller*.

4 Which word means *many* and *very*?

5 What does the word **lawn** mean?

6 How would you say *I would like five of those*?

7 Which of these phrases means *the smallest shirt*? **'amiiS aSghar; aSghar 'amiiS**.

8 What is the feminine of the colour **aHmar**?

9 How do you say *I'll take them*?

10 If **alwaan taanya** means *other colours*, how would you say *other postcards*?

Now check whether you can:

- ask how much something costs
- understand currencies used in the Arab World
- ask for an item in a shop
- ask if you can look at something
- ask if you can try something on
- explain that something is too big, small or expensive
- ask for a smaller/bigger size
- ask for different colours
- bargain on a price

Word association can double the amount of vocabulary you retain. For example, you could link in your mind words in similar categories, such as **kart** and **Taabi9**, or **shaay** and **'ahwa**. When you learn an adjective, learn any obvious opposite as well: **kibiir** and **Saghiir**, **rakhiiS** and **ghaali**.

Checkpoint 2

1 **2•35** You ask the receptionist at the Cedarland Hotel in Beirut about visiting three places you need to get to. Listen and make a note of where each one is and how long it would take to get there from the hotel.

	where?	how far?
a maT9am kebabji *Kebabji Restaurant*	....	....
b il-jaami9a il-amriikiyya *The American University*	....	....
c il-matHaf il-waTani *The National Museum*	....	....

2 **2•36** You now need to know which days these three places are open. Listen to the receptionist and fill in the table:

	Open	Closed
maT9am kebabji		
il-jaami9a il-amriikiyya		
il-matHaf il-waTani		

3 Select which phrase you might use:

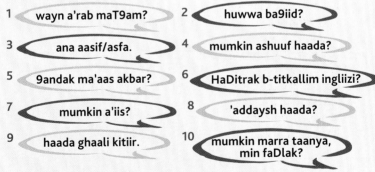

1 wayn a'rab maT9am?

2 huwwa ba9iid?

3 ana aasif/asfa.

4 mumkin ashuuf haada?

5 9andak ma'aas akbar?

6 HaDitrak b-titkallim ingliizi?

7 mumkin a'iis?

8 'addaysh haada?

9 haada ghaali kitiir.

10 mumkin marra taanya, min faDlak?

a to find out if someone speaks English. **b** to ask to try something on.

c to ask where the nearest restaurant is. **d** to ask for a larger size.

e to ask if you can look at something. **f** to say that it's very expensive.

g to get someone to repeat what they have said. **h** to ask how much something costs.

i to say you are sorry. **j** to ask if somewhere is far.

4 Group the following words into seven groups of three words.

> mi'aabil   ruuH   finjaan   9ala Tuul   isharb
> maktab bariid   arba9miyya   Siniyya   liff
> janb   'amiiS   talatmiyya   maHaTTa
> 9al-yasaar   9al-yamiin   matHaf   ibrii'
> miitayn   fustaan   waraa   khud

5 Find the correct word to make a match

a	finjaan	1	aHmar
b	jariida	2	zar'a
c	shanTa	3	il-bariid
d	maHaTTat	4	il-madiina
e	maktab	5	shaay
f	wasaT	6	il-qiTaar
g	fustaan	7	ingliiziyya

6 2•37 Listen to the prices for the following items in a Syrian **suu'** and write them down.

	L.S.
coffee pot	
English newspaper	
6 cups	
Arabic tray	
shirt	
scarf	

7 Which questions would you ask to receive the following answers?

a .... aywa b-atkallam ingliizi shwayya.

b .... a'rab Saydaliyya khamsamiit mitr min hawn.

c .... laa', il-maHaTTa ba9iida min hawn.

d .... il-bank maftuuH min is-saa9a tis9a lis-saa9a waaHda.

e .... haada bi sittiin dinaar.

f .... maa fiih suubermarket hawn.

8 Fill the gaps in these sentences using the words in the box:

1 **haadi-S Siniyya** .... **kitiir.**

2 **miitayn wa khamsiin lira** ....?

3 **mumkin** .... **haada-l fustaan law samaHti?**

4 **shuu** .... **taman?**

5 .... **aruuH lil-maHaTTa?**

6 **ruuH 9ala Tuul wa ba9dayn** .... **yamiin.**

7 .... **awwal shaari9 9al-yasaar.**

| aHsan | kiif | ghaalya | a'iis | liff | mniiH | khud |

9 **2•38** Listen to four people being given directions from Café France in Casablanca. Follow their route on the map and write down in English the place they're going to and the number which corresponds to it on the map. You'll hear **na9am**, which is another way of saying *yes*.

1 ....   2 ....

3 ....   4 ....

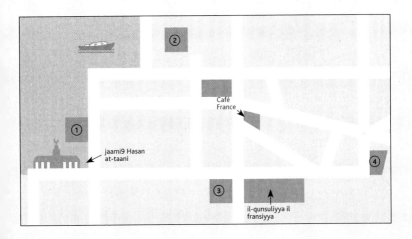

10 Complete the descriptions next to each pair of items using an appropriate word from the list. Here **min** means *than*.

a aSghar	b akbar	c aghla	d arkhaS

1 il-fustaan il-azra' .... min il-fustaan il-aHmar.

2 ish-shanTa il-Hamra .... min ish-shanTa il khaDra.

3 is-sayyaara il-bayDa .... min is-sayyaara il-zar'a.

4 il-kitaab il-aswad ....min il-kitaab il-aSfar.

11 Look at this shopping list. Put 1 by the ones you would buy in a **ba'aal**; 2 in a **kushk** and 3 in a **suu'**

a majalla ☐	b tuffaaH ☐	c fanaajiin ☐
d Siniyya ☐	e jariida ☐	f burtu'aan ☐
g ibrii' 'ahwa ☐	h shammaam ☐	i kuruut ☐

9andak ghurfa?

finding a suitable hotel room

... and saying how long you want to stay

checking in at the hotel

making requests

In the Arab world there's a wide range of hotels which are generally known as **fundu'**, although the word **utiil** is used in many Arab countries as well.

Hotels range from small family run outfits to the most luxurious **saba9 nujuum** *seven-star* hotels of Dubai. Breakfast in the smaller hotels is normally French style, particularly in Egypt, North Africa and the Levant. Staying in the older ex-colonial type of hotel in the Arab world can be delightful but it's advisable to check whether the room has **takyiif** *air-conditioning* in the summer months as not all rooms are equipped with this.

Guests will often be asked to leave their **jawaaz safar** *passport* at reception overnight as visitors need to be registered with the local police and this is normally done by the hotel.

Finding a suitable hotel room

1 **2●39** Listen to the key language:

9andak/9andik ghurfa?	Do you have a room? (to m/f)
biddi ghurfa li shakhS waaHid/	I want a room for one person/
li shakhSayn.	for two people.
bi Hammaam/fuTuur/	with a bathroom/breakfast/
takyiif	air-conditioning
li kam shakhS?	For how many people?
li talaat ashkhaaS.	For three people.
'addaysh il-layla?	How much is it a night?
il-layla bi miyya wa khamsiin lira.	It's 150 Syrian pounds per night.

---

bil 9arabi ...

to say *two* of something, a special form called the dual is used. It's made by adding **-ayn** onto the end of the noun. If the noun ends with **-a** then **-tayn** is added: **shakhS** *a person*, **shakh<u>Sayn</u>** *two people*; **layla** *a night*, **layl<u>tayn</u>** *two nights*. The dual form is not used when ordering food or drinks.   **G20**

---

2 **2●40** Listen to some people asking about rooms at the Baron Hotel in Aleppo. Tick what kind of accommodation they want.

Sami Ayyoub

Sonya Brett

Mohammed Bakry

Miriam Haddad

3 **2●41** Listen as Sami now enquires about the prices. Jot down what the price is per night with and without breakfast.

... and saying how long you want to stay

1 **2•42** Listen to the key language:

li kam layla?	For how many nights?
biddi anzil ...	I want to stay for ...
... layltayn/talaat layaali/	... two nights/three nights/
haadi-l layla bass.	just tonight *Lit*. this night only.
<u>**aymta**</u> **biddak tinzil/biddik tinzili?**	**When** do you want to stay? (to m/f)
min il-yawm li yawm it-talaata	from today until Tuesday
min yawm waaHid sitta li talaata sitta	from the 1ˢᵗ of June to the 3ʳᵈ of June
aasif/asfa, il-fundu' kullu maHjuuz.	Sorry (m/f), the hotel is full.

2 **2•43** Listen as guests say how long they want to stay at the Sham Palace Hotel in Damascus. From the list below number the three you hear in the order you hear them:

haadi-l layla bass

talaat layaali

min il-yawm li yawm it-talaata

min il-yawm li yawm il-jum9a

layltayn

---

bil 9arabi ...

the names for months can differ from region to region in the Arabic-speaking world. It is becoming increasingly common to hear numbers being used instead. The number of the day comes first, followed directly by the number of the month: **yawm waaHid sitta** *1 June* Lit. *day 1/6;* **yawm tis9a 9ashara** *9 October* Lit. *day 9/10*. These can also mean *on 1 June, on 9 October*.

---

3 **2•44** The receptionist at the Ummayad Hotel is taking some bookings over the phone. Listen and note when the three callers want rooms. Which caller cannot be accommodated?

a .... b .... c ....

Checking in at the hotel

1 **2•45** Listen to the key language:

9andi Hajz.	I have a reservation.
Hajazt/Hajazti aymta?	When did you book? (to m/f)
Hajazt imbaariH.	I booked yesterday.
jawaaz safarak/safarik,	Please give me your passport.
min faDlak/min faDlik.	(to m/f)
imla/imli il-istimaara,	Please fill in the form. (to m/f)
min faDlak/min faDlik.	
itfaDDal/itfaDDali il-muftaaH.	Here's your key. (to m/f)
il-asinsiir fiT <u>T</u>aabi' il-awwal/	The lift is on the first/second/
it-taani/it-taalit.	third <u>floor</u>.

---

bil 9arabi ...

the past tense uses suffixes which are added to the verb, as opposed to prefixes, which are used in the present tense: **aHjiz** *I book,* **Hajazt** *I booked.* **tiHjiz** *you book* (m), **Hajazt** *you booked* (m). **tiHjizi** *you book* (f), **Hajazti** *you booked* (f). **G9–11**

---

2 **2•46** Listen to a visitor checking in the Sindibad Hotel in Rabat and tick the correct options. You'll hear **ghurfa raqm** *room number*.

a She's booked a   single   double   double with bath

b She's staying for   two nights   three nights   four nights

c She's asked   for her passport   to fill in the form
                if she wants breakfast

d Her room number is   110   220   210

3 **2•46** Listen again, what was the problem with her booking?

4 **2•47** Listen to someone else checking in, and complete the details of their booking on the form opposite. Then listen again to find out:

a which floor the room on
b where the lift is.

> **ism:** ....
> **min:** .... **li:** ....
> **jawaaz raqm:** ....
> **jinsiyya:** ....
> **ghurfa raqm:** ....

Making requests

1   **2•48** Listen to the key language:

mumkin ...	Can ...
... akhalli shanTati hawn?	... I leave my suitcase here?
... adfa9 bi haada-l kart?	... I pay with this card?
... asta9mil Hammaam is-sibaaHa?	... I use the swimming pool?
... ashuuf il-mudiir?	... I see the manager?
... tuTlub/tuTlubi taksi 9ashaani?	... you order a taxi for me? (to m/f)
akiid	certainly

2   **2•49** Maryam Munir is about to check out of the Sindibad Hotel. Listen to what she says to the receptionist Hasan Abaaza and make a note in English of the two things she asks for:

a ……………………….. b …………………………………

What do you think **ayy khidma taanya** means?

---

bil 9arabi ...

mumkin is used with the present tense without the **b**-prefix. As well as being used to mean *Can I?* as in **mumkin adfa9?** *Can I pay?* it is also used when politely asking someone to do something:
mumkin tuTlub/tuTlubi ...? *Can you order/request ....?* (to m/f)
mumkin ti'uul li/ti'uuli li ...? *Can you tell me ....?* (to m/f).   **G17**

---

3   **2•50** The guests are keeping Hasan Abaaza busy with their requests. Listen and match the guests with what they want.

Mrs Campbell	use the swimming pool
Dr Rushdi	leave his suitcase here
Mr Ramzi	see the manager
Miss Buthayna	pay with this card

4   **2•50** Listen to the conversations again. Which request could Hasan Abaaza not agree to? Why not?

put it all together

Hajazt imbaariH.	bi takyiif
9andi Hajz.	'addaysh il-layla?
9andik ghurfa?	biddi anzil haadi-l layla bass.
mumkin asta9mil Hammaam is-sibaaHa?	

1   Which phrase from the box would you use to:

   a   ask if there's a room available

   b   say with air-conditioning

   c   say you want to stay tonight only

   d   say you have a reservation

   e   ask the price per night

   f   ask if you can use the swimming pool

   g   say you booked yesterday

2   Complete the following:

   a **9andak ghurfa li** .... ?

   b **biddi ghurfa li** .... **bi** ....

   c **biddi ghurfa bi** ....

   d **mumkin** .... **9ashaani?**

   e **mumkin** .... ?

3   Say these dates in Arabic:

   a 31 January   b 24 December

   c 5 March   d 8 July

1   **2•51** You're at the Shepheard's Hotel in Amman looking for a room for one night.

- **marHaba. ayy khidma?**
- Ask if they have a room available.
- **biddak tinzil li kam layla?**
- Say for one night only.
- **li shakhS waaHid?**
- Say no, say you want a double with a bathroom.
- **aywa, fiih ghurfa bi saba9iin dinaar il-layla.**
- Ask if breakfast is included.
- **aywa, bi fuTuur.**

2   **2•52** The following morning you're ready to check out.

- **SabaaH il-khayr.**
- Say good morning to her.
- **ayy khidma?**
- Ask for the bill.
- **raqm il-ghurfa law samaHt?**
- Say you're in room 210.
- **saba9iin dinaar, min faDlak.**
- Ask if you can pay with this card.
- **aywa, Tab9an.**
- Ask if you can leave your suitcase there until 4 o'clock today.
- **aywa, akiid. b-ashuufak ba9dayn.**
- Say goodbye.

quiz

1 Which is the odd one out? **layla**, **yawm**, **layltayn**, **ghurfa**.

2 In a hotel how would you say *I want to stay for four nights*?

3 What is the Arabic for *7 October*?

4 Who is **il-mudiir** in a hotel?

5 How would say *a room with air-conditioning*?

6 Would you use **mumkin tuTlubi taksi 9ashaani?** or **mumkin tuTlub taksi 9ashaani?** to ask a man to call a taxi for you?

7 What do you do if you hear **imla il-istimaara**?

8 If you're given **il-muftaaH** what do you have?

9 How would you ask for two rooms?

Now check whether you can …

- ask if there's a room available
- specify what kind of room, with bathroom/breakfast/air-conditioning
- ask how much it costs per night
- say how long you want accommodation for, giving precise dates
- say you've booked a room
- ask if you can do something, e.g. leave your suitcase
- ask someone to do something for you

When learning a language it can be easy to underestimate how much you know. Go back to the early units to prove to yourself how much you've learnt. Think also about what you find easy … and difficult. If you can identify your strengths and weaknesses, you can shape your own learning.

Arabic script: numbers

Many Arab countries outside North Africa use written numerals known as the Hindi or Persian numerals. These read from left to right as in English and are as follows.

0	1	2	3	4	5	6	7	8	9	10
٠	١	٢	٣	٤	٥	٦	٧	٨	٩	١٠

1 Can you read the distances in kilometres كم of the following places as marked on the Damascus-Aleppo Motorway?

airport ....

Homs ....

Hama ....

Aleppo ....

المطار ٢٦ كم

حمص ٢١٠ كم

حمـاة ٣٣٠ كم

حلـب ٤٤٦ كم

2 You have been given a business card by Nabil Nisnaas. Write in English the telephone numbers, which are presented on the card in the following order:

1 home

....

2 office

....

3 mobile

....

الاسم : **نبيل نسناس**

رقم التلفون: البيت: ٠٥٣٣٢٨٦٢٨٤٤

المكتب: ٠٥٣٣١٧٤٦١٦١

الموبيل: ٠٦٢٥٧١٨٨٩٩٢

Check your answers on page 90.

Arabic script: answers

Arabic script: 1

2 انا البيت بريطانيا
امس سيارة عمان

3 1 c, I /I am; 2 f, daughter/girl;
3 e, father; 4 b, my son; 5 d, door,
gate; 6 g, girls; 7 a, two

Arabic script: 2

2 مكتب سلام شمس
محطة المغرب امس

3 salaam *peace*
4 1 b, king; 2 c, sun; 3 a, office; 4 d,
book

Arabic script: 3

2 مدرسة سيارة يسار
رقم عربي

Right to left: madrasa *school,*
sayyaara *car,* yasaar *left,* raqm
number, 9arabi *Arabic*

3 1 f; 2 h; 3 e; 4 g; 5 d; 6 b; 7 a; 8 c
4 1 d; 2 e; 3 b; 4 c; 5 a
5 1 as-suudaan *Sudan;* 2 suuriya
Syria.

Arabic script: 4

2 هناك هذه سهل
مهندس هذا اسمه

3 *a school*
4 1 d; 2 a; 3 b; 4 c
5 1 e; 2 a; 3 d

Arabic script: 5

2 مطار طلب مطعم
قطار فطور

Right to left: maTaar *airport,*
Talab *request,* maT9am
restaurant, qiTaar *train,* fuTuur
breakfast

3 *Abu Dhabi*
4 1 10.40; 2 Rabat; 3 departing;
4 no

Arabic script: 6

2 عندي مصنع
عمل نعم مطعم شارع

3 shaay bi na9na9 *d;* 9aSiir 9inab *c*
4 2 a; 1 c; 3 d; 4 b
5 *3 is correct.* 1 shaari9 lubnaan; 2
shaari9 9abd al-9aziiz; 4 shaari9
al-Hamraa'

Arabic script: 7

2 1 e; 2 a; 3 d; 4 c; 5 b
3 *On shop doors.* 1 maqfuul *closed;*
2 maftuuH *open.*
4 1 f; 2 c; 3 g; 4 b; 5 d; 6 e; 7 a

The hamza

1 1 c; 2 f; 3 a; 4 e; 5 b; 6 d
2 1 e; 2 a; 3 b; 4 c; 5 d
3 ad-daar al-bayDaa' *Casablanca*

Numbers

1 *Airport 26km; Homs 210km;
Hama 330km; Aleppo 446km*
2 *House: 05332862844; office:
05331746161; mobile: 0625
7188992*

fiih qiTaar li Halab?

saying where you're going

asking about public transport

buying tickets

checking travel times

The majority of foreign visitors to the Arab world use public transport to travel between cities. For travel within cities use taxis; they're great places to practise your Arabic!

qiTaaraat *trains* are generally clean, efficient and inexpensive as they're often government owned. Networks vary in size and in some Arab countries there is virtually no network at all. Generally **daraja uula** *first class* is good value as it is usually air-conditioned and refreshments are available.

To explore scenic parts of Arab countries not served by public transport you can take a **sayyaara mu'ajjara** *hire car*. You can often get a better rate locally but you need to make sure prices include **ta'miin** *insurance*.

Saying where you're going

1 **2•53** Listen to the key language:

biddi aruuH li ba9albak il-yawm.	I want to go to Baalbek today.
raayiH/raayHa lil-maTaar bukra.	I'm going to the airport tomorrow. (m/f)
HaDirtak raayiH/HaDirtik raayHa aymta?	When are you going? (to m/f)
laazim taakhud/taakhdi taksi.	You must take a taxi. (to m/f)
mumkin aakhud il-qiTaar?	Can I take the train?
mumkin tiruuH/tiruuHi ...	You can go ... (to m/f)
... bil baaS/bil qiTaar.	... by bus/by train.

---

bil 9arabi ...

raayiH/raayHa (m/f) *going* is an active participle like **saakin/ saakna** *living* (see page 20). It's used a lot in spoken Arabic, and in the Levant is followed by the preposition li. **G12**

---

2 **2•54** A guest at the Safir Hotel in Beirut is asking the receptionist about different ways to get to Baalbek. You will hear **qiTaaraat** *trains*.

Tick the modes of transport which are available:

3 **2•55** A visitor to Amman asks how he can get from his hotel to the airport. Listen and number their conversation in the order you hear it.

raayiH lil maTaar bukra. mumkin aakhud il-baaS min hawn?

Hawaali arba9iin dinaar.

SabaaH in-nuur.

laa', maa fiih baaS lil-maTaar. laazim taakhud taksi.

'addaysh it-taksi min hawn lil-maTaar?

haada ghaali kitiir!

SabaaH il-khayr.

4 How would you say the following?
   ● I want to go to the museum. ● Can I take the bus?

Asking about public transport

1   2•56 Listen to the key language:

haada-l baaS b-yruuH li 9ammaan?	Does this bus go to Amman?
min wayn b-yruuH?	Where does it go from?
ayy raqm baaS?	Which number bus?
'addaysh b-yaakhud?	How long does it take? (m)
'addaysh b-taakhud ir-riHla?	How long does the journey take? (f)
b-yaakhud/b-taakhud ...	It takes ... (m/f)
... saa9a waaHda/saa9atayn.	... 1 hour/2 hours.
... arba9 saa9aat.	... 4 hours.

---

bil 9arabi ...

yaakhud *to take* is used when talking about the time something takes. The masculine **b-yaakhud** is used in a general sense: **b-yaakhud 9ashar da'aayi'** *it takes 10 minutes*; while the feminine **b-taakhud** is used when referring to a specific feminine noun: **ir-riHla b-taakhud ...** *the journey* (f) *takes ...*   **G1, G20**

---

2   2•57 Linda is at the **maHaTTat il-baaSaat** *bus station* in Damascus. Listen and decide whether the following statements are true or false.

	True	False
a This bus is going to the university.		
b No 32 bus goes to the Umayyad Mosque.		
c The journey takes twenty minutes.		
d There isn't a bus to the airport from here.		

3   2•58 Linda is going to go on some long distance bus journeys. Listen and write down how long they take. You'll hear **hunaak** *over there*.

a Damascus-Aleppo ....

b Damascus-Amman ....

c Damascus-Homs ....

4   2•58 Listen again and note down where the buses to Aleppo and Homs go from.

Buying tickets

1 **2•59** Listen to the key language:

biddi tazkartayn li dimashq,	I'd like two tickets for
min faDlak/min faDlik.	Damascus, please. (to m/f)
daraja <u>uula</u>/daraja <u>taanya</u>	<u>first</u>/<u>second</u> class
ruuHa	single
ruuHa raj9a	return
tazkarat ruuHa raj9a	a return ticket
ayy raSiif?	Which platform?

---

bil 9arabi ...

nouns change depending on whether they are singular or plural, if they are used with numbers, and if they are used with another noun:

tazkara *ticket,* **tazkartayn** *2 tickets,* **tazaakir** *3–10 tickets e.g.* **khams tazaakir** *5 tickets,* **tazkarat ruuHa** *a single ticket.*   **G1, G20**

---

2 **2•60** Mark Jones is booking train tickets at Aleppo station. Listen to the conversation and complete the travel information below. You'll hear **alaaf**, which is used to count thousands.

No. of tickets .... Class ....

Type of ticket (single/return) .... Destination ....

Day of travel .... Total ticket price ....

3 **2•60** Listen again and write down which platform he needs to go to.

4 **2•61** Listen to four people buying train tickets at Casablanca station. Match the tickets with the prices as you hear them:

a a single to Rabat   b two return tickets to Al-Jadida

c three singles tickets to Fez   d a single to the airport

12 dirhams	25 dirhams	45 dirhams	120 dirhams

Checking travel times

1 **2•62** Listen to the key language:

ayy saa9a ...	What time ...
... il-qiTaar li Tanja?	... is the train to Tangiers?
... b-yimshi?	... does it leave? (m)
... b-yuSal marraaksh?	... does it arrive at Marrakesh? (m)
is-saa9a tamanya wa nuSS.	At 8.30. *Lit*. The time is eight thirty.
aymta il-qiTaar il-jaay?	When is the next train?
ba9d ...	In ...
... rub9 saa9a.	... a quarter of an hour.
... nuSS saa9a/saa9a.	... half an hour/an hour.

bil 9arabi ...

the hour is divided into: **nuSS** *a half,* **rub9** *a quarter,* **tult** *a third* (i.e. 20 minutes). Telling the time between the hours is done by either adding the word **wa** *plus* or **illa** *minus*: **9ashara wa nuSS** 10.30, **9ashara wa rub9** 10.15, **9ashara wa tult** 10.20. **9ashara illa rub9** 9.45, **9ashara illa tult** 9.40, **9ashara wa khamsa** 10.05, **9ashara illa 9ashara** 9.50.

25 past and 25 to the hour are calculated from the half hour: **talaata wa nuSS illa khamsa** 3.25 Lit. 3.30 *minus* 5. **arba9a wa nuSS wa khamsa** 4.35 Lit. 4.30 *and* 5.

2 **2•63** Listen to a conversation at Rabat train station. You'll hear the word **ya9ni** meaning *I mean* or *you mean*.

a At what time does the next train to Tangiers leave?
b How much time does the passenger have before the train leaves?
c At what time does the train arrive at Tangiers?

3 **2•64** Listen to people at Casablanca station checking train times and fill in the departure and arrival times:

	idh-dhahaab *departure*	**il-wuSuul** *arrival*
marraaksh *Marrakesh*		
Tanja *Tangiers*		
il-jadiida *Al-Jadida*		

4 How would you ask when the next train to Rabat is?

put it all together

1   Match the times with the clocks:

1 `02.25` 2 `10.30` 3 `08.35`

4 `04.45` 5 `06.10` 6 `11.55`

a is-saa9a 9ashara wa nuSS   b is-saa9a sitta wa 9ashara

c is-saa9a itnaashar illa   d is-saa9a itnayn wa nuSS
   khamsa   illa khamsa

e is-saa9a khamsa illa rub9   f is-saa9a tamanya wa
                                    nuSS wa khamsa

2   Say these times in Arabic:

a 7.30   b 12.45   c 2.15   d 3.25   e 4.20   f 9.50

3   Choose the correct verb from the box for each of the
    following questions:

1   aymta .... il-qiTaar min Tanja?

2   mumkin .... il-baaS?

3   ayy is-saa9a .... il-qiTaar il-jaay li Halab?

4   'addaysh .... ir-riHla min hawn li ba9albak?

5   laazim .... taksi, ya madaam.

6   mumkin .... bil qiTaar li dimaashq, ya sayyid.

> b-taakhud   tiruuH   b-yuSal
>
> b-yimshi   taakhdi   aakhud

4   Match the following words to form pairs.

a tazkarat   1 saa9aat
b maHaTTat   2 raqm itnayn
c daraja   3 il-jaay
d raSiif   4 il-qiTaar
e il-qiTaar   5 uula
f khams   6 ruuHa

1   **2•65** You are at the Abdalleh bus station in Amman and want to go to Damascus.

- Ask the woman at the ticket office if there's a bus to Damascus.
- ◆ **aywa, fiih baaS li dimashq kull yawm is-saa9a talaata.**
- Ask her how long the journey takes.
- ◆ **ir-riHla b-taakhud Hawaali arba9 saa9aat min 9ammaan li dimashq.**
- Ask her how much a ticket costs.
- ◆ **biddak tazkarat ruuHa aw ruuHa raj9a?**
- Tell her you'd like two single tickets please.
- ◆ **Tayyib, haada khamsiin dinaar, min faDlak.**
- Say here you are.
- ◆ **shukran.**

2   **2•66** You are now in Damascus and would like to take the train to Aleppo.

- Ask the man in the ticket office when the next train leaves for Aleppo.
- ◆ **b-yimshi is-saa9a tamanya wa nuSS.**
- Find out what time the train arrives in Aleppo.
- ◆ **b-yuSal is-saa9a itnaa9sh wa nuSS.**
- Say you'd like a return ticket.
- ◆ **daraja taanya aw daraja uula?**
- Say first class please. Ask how much it is.
- ◆ **tamanmiit lira.**
- Ask the price of second class.
- ◆ **sittmiyya wa khamsiin lira.**
- Say you would like one return ticket, first class.
- ◆ **itfaDDal. riHla sa9iida.** (*Bon Voyage*)
- Thank him, and ask which platform the train goees from.
- ◆ **raSiif raqm itnayn.**

quiz

1 Is **tis9a illa tult** 8.40, 9.20 or 9.40?
2 Which word means *journey/trip/flight*?
3 How do you say *second class return ticket*?
4 What's the difference between **is-saa9a arba9** and **arba9 saa9aat**?
5 What does **il-jaay** mean?
6 Where are you most likely to see a **raSiif**?
7 How do you say *two tickets* in Arabic?
8 What's the difference between **laazim takkhud taksi** and **mumkin taakhud taksi**.

Now check whether you can ...

- say where you're going/you want to go
- ask if there are buses or trains
- find out when a bus/train leaves
- ask how long it takes to get to a place
- buy train tickets
- understand the time of day

You can use the internet to plan real or hypothetical journeys. You can practise what you've just learnt – work out what questions you'd need to ask to see if journeys are possible, and to find out prices and what time trains and buses leave and arrive. riHla sa9iida!

Modern Standard Arabic

The language used for writing and formal speech is known as Modern Standard Arabic (MSA). It is referred to in Arabic as **fuS-Ha** and is derived from Classical Arabic, the language of the Qur'an. You'll see MSA on signs and notices, in books, newspapers and magazines. MSA is not used in everyday interaction; although Arabic speakers might use it for formal discussions, they don't use it to speak to someone on an informal basis. As a visitor to the Arab world, the only time you're likely to hear it is if you watch the news on television or listen to announcements at stations and airports.

Spoken or colloquial Arabic **9amiyya** is the language used in everyday life. It varies from region to region but can be divided into five major dialects: Maghrebi (spoken in North Africa), Egyptian, Iraqi, Gulf and Levantine (spoken in Lebanon, Syria, Jordan and Palestine).

MSA and the regional dialects have many similarities. They tend to differ in the more everyday words and expressions. Below are some common differences:

What?

		What's your name?
Levantine	**shuu**	**shuu ismak/ismik?**
Gulf	**aysh**	**aysh ismak?**
Egyptian	**eeh**	**ismak eeh?**
MSA	**maa***	**maa ismuka/ismuki?**

* **maadha** before a verb: **maadha turiid?** *What would you like?* (to m)

The

		the house
Levantine and most spoken dialects	**il**	**il-bayt**
MSA	**al**	**al-bayt**

How much/how many?

	How much?	*How many?*
Levantine	**addaysh?**	**kam?**
Egyptian, Gulf	**bi kam?**	**kam?**
Moroccan	**bishHaal?**	**shHaal min?**
MSA	**bi kam?**	**kam?**

Want/would like

To say *want/would like*, Levantine Arabic uses: **biddi** *I want*, **biddak/ik** *you* (m/f) *want*, **biddu/ha** *he/she wants*
and Egyptian: **9aawiz** *I/you* (m)/*he want(s)*, **9aawza** *I/you* (f)/*she want(s)*
MSA uses the verb **yuriidu**:

uriid *I want/would like*	**yuriid** *he wants/would like*
turiid *you* (m) *want/would like*	**turiid** *she wants/would like*
turiidiin *you* (f) *want/would like*	

There is/there are

		there's a restaurant
Levantine, Egyptian and Gulf	**fiih**	**fiih maT9am**
Moroccan	**kayn**	**kayn maT9am**
MSA	**hunaaka**	**hunaaka maT9am**

Asking questions

Most Arabic spoken dialects including Levantine use intonation when asking questions which require a yes or no answer, whereas MSA prefixes the question with the word **hal**:
b-tHibb is-samak? → **hal tuHibb as-samak?** *Do you like fish?*

Not

In spoken Arabic, *not* is **mish** or **maa** (see G18 page 138):
ana mish min lubnaan. *I'm not from Lebanon.*
maa b-a9raf *I don't know.*

MSA has the verb **laysa** meaning *am/is/are not*:
lastu min lubnaan. *I'm not from Lebanon.*
lasta/lasti min al-urdun. *You* (m/f) *are not from Jordan.*
laysa/laysat mudarris/mudarrisa. *He's/she's not a teacher.*

Otherwise **laa** is used: **laa a9rif** *I don't know.*

In Egypt, North Africa and parts of the Levant, **-sh** is added to certain negative structures:
maa fiih → **mafiish** *there isn't*
maa b-ashrab → **ma b-ashrabsh** *I don't drink*

il-akl laziiz!

understanding the menu

saying what you like and don't like

ordering a meal

expressing appreciation

Arabic food is really delicious and appeals to most people owing to its variety and sheer tastiness. One of the best-known aspects of Lebanese food is the **muqabbilaat** *starters* or **mazza** *mezze*, many of which are **nabaati** *vegetarian* and served with warm **khubz 9arabi** *pitta bread*.

Main courses are often **mashwiyyaat** *charcoal-grilled food,* such as **laHma** *meat*, **samak** *fish or* **dajaaj** *chicken,* which are popular throughout the Arab world. In Morocco the smell of the grilled meat and the aroma of the mint tea together is truly memorable. From vegetable couscous in the West to **betinjaan maHshi** *stuffed aubergines* in the East, there is always an alternative to meat. Although potatoes are eaten, rice is the staple food in the East whereas in North Africa it is couscous or bread.

For dessert many Arabs prefer a selection of **fawaakih** *fruit* after their meals. However the Arab world is famous for its **Hilu** *sweetmeats,* many of which contain honey, different types of nuts and filo pastry. There are also milk puddings flavoured with **ma' zaher** *rose water*.

Understanding the menu

1   2•67 Look at **il-lista** *the menu* below. Listen to the waiter and tick the items he mentions from the menu. You'll hear **9andnaa** *we have*. What items aren't mentioned?

Lebanese salads and starters	السـلطات اللبنانية والمقبلات	is-salaaTaat il-lubnaaniyya w-il muqabbilaat
smoked aubergine dip	متبل	mutabbal
beans	فول	fuul
falafel	فلافل	falaafil
crushed wheat & parsley salad	تبولة	tabbuuleh
charcoal grilled dishes	اطباق المشـويات على الفحم	aTbaaq il-mashwiyyaat 9al-faHm
grilled lamb or beef	كفتة	kufta mashwiyya
grilled liver	كبدة	kibda mashwiyya
grilled chicken	دجاج	dajaaj mashwi
grilled fish	سمك	samak mashwi
mixed grill	مشـوي مشـكل	mashwi mishakkal
desserts	الحلو	il-Hilu
crème caramel	كريم كرامل	krim karamil
milk pudding	أم علي	umm 9ali
baklava	بقلاوة	ba'laawa
rice pudding	رز بحليب	ruzz bi Haliib
melted cheese covered with hot noodles	كنافة	kunaafa

2   2•68 Farida is ready to order. Listen and make a note in English of the starters and main courses she asks for.

....

3   2•69 After the main course, Hiba asks about dessert. What does she want? What does she order? Listen out for **9andkum**? *Do you have?* (plural)

Saying what you like and don't like

1   2•70 Listen to the key language:

b-tHibb/b-tHibbi il-kibbeh?	Do you like meat rissoles? (to m/f)
b-aHibbu.	I like it. (m)
b-aHibbha.	I like it (f)/them.
b-aHibb is-samak.	I like fish.
maa b-aHibb il-falaafil.	I don't like falafel.
b-afaDDil id-dajaaj.	I prefer chicken.
b-taakul/b-taakli laHma?	Do you eat meat? (to m/f)
maa b-aakul laHma <u>abadan</u>.	I <u>never</u> eat meat.

bil 9arabi ...

The verb to like is **yiHibb**: **b-aHibb** *I like*, **b-tHibb** *you like* (m),
b-tHibbi *you like* (f).

To make a general statement you use the definite article, e.g.
b-aHibb is-samak. *I like fish*. Lit. *I like the fish*.

2   2•71 Hasan Shoukry has invited Mark Jones out for dinner in
Damascus. Listen and put a tick next to the foods Mark likes and a
cross next to those he doesn't like.

falaafil   kibbeh   laHma   samak   ba'laawa   kunaafa

3   2•72 Farida is checking what type of food her students David and
Jacqueline like before ordering them lunch in Beirut. Listen and fill in
the gaps. You'll hear **ya9ni** which means *so-so* in this context.

- ya Jacqueline, ... il-kufta il-mashwiyya?
- ya9ni, mish kitiir .... id-dajaaj.
- w-inta, ya David, ... il-kufta il-mashwiyya?
- laa', ana nabaati, maa b-aakul laHma .... !
- Tayyib. .... is-salaaTaat il-lubaaniyya?
- Tab9an, ... kitiir.

What do you think **nabaati** means?

4   Practise saying what foods you like using **b-aHibb**.

Ordering a meal

1   **2•73** Listen to the key language:

ayy naw9 ...	What kind of ...
... Hilu 9andkum?	... desserts do you have?
... akl nabaati 9andkum?	... vegetarian food do you have?
biddna Taawila li itnayn/arba9.	We'd like a table for two/four.
il-akl hawn <u>kwayyis</u> kitiir.	The food here is very <u>good</u>.
haada kullu.	That's all.
mumkin kamaan khubz,	More bread please. *Lit*. Is it
law samaHt/ samaHti?	possible more bread, please?

---

bil 9arabi ...

there are two ways of asking a question with *what:*

- **ayy** followed by a noun, indicating that there are options: **ayy naw9?** *What/which kind?* **ayy Hilu?** *What/which dessert?* **ayy lawn?** *What/which colour?*
- **shuu** followed by a noun or a verb: **shuu b-taakhud/b-taakhdi?** *What are you having?* **shuu ismak/ismik?** *What is your name?*

---

2   **2•74** Ayman Shihadeh is ordering food for some conference delegates at the Abu Muusa grill in Irbid. Note how many of each dish he orders.

dajaaj mashwi	**mutabbal**
kibda mashwiyya	**SalSat TaHiina** *sesame paste*
mashwi mishakkal	**mujaddara** *rice with lentils*

What else does he ask for?

3   **2•75** Nadia Rif'at has invited her friend Khalid to her favourite restaurant in Amman. Listen to the conversation.

a   Why does Nadia like this restaurant so much?
b   Which two desserts are suggested by the waitress?
c   What is not available today?
d   What does Nadia say when asked **biddik shi taani**?

4   How would you say the following:

- What type of **fawaakih** *fruit* have you got?
- I'd like two mixed grills please.
- I'll have one aubergine dip and one rice with lentils.

Expressing appreciation

1   2•76 Listen to the key language:

kiif <u>kaan</u> il-akl?	How <u>was</u> the food?
il-akl kaan laziiz.	The food was delicious.
khuSuuSan il-falaafil	especially the falafel
il-khidma kaanat mumtaaza <u>fi9lan</u>.	The service was <u>really</u> excellent.
il-garsawn kaan <u>laTiif</u> jiddan.	The waiter was very <u>nice</u>.
il-aanisa kaan laTiifa jiddan.	The waitress was very nice.

---

bil 9arabi ...

there's no verb *to be* in the present tense: *I am in Beirut* is simply **ana fi bayruut**. Lit. *I in Beirut*. However, the verb *to be* exists in the past: **kunt** *I was,* **kaan** *he/it was,* **kunt/kunti** *you were* (m/f), **kaanat** *she/it was* and *they were* (f). **(ana) kunt fi bayruut**. *I was in Beirut.*   **G15**

---

2   2•77 Farida asks David and Jacqueline about their food. Listen and answer the following:

a Which dish did David like in particular?
b What impressed Jacqueline?
c What is Farida's final question to Jacqueline?

3   2•78 Back at the Abu Muusa restaurant the manager asks if his guests have enjoyed the food. Listen and note down in Arabic the answers to his questions.

- **kiif kaan il-akl?**

- ....

- ....

- **wa kiif kaanat il-khidma?**

- ....

- **w-il garsawn?**

- ....

4   In Arabic how would you say:

- the food was delicious, especially the grilled chicken.

put it all together

1   Which of the following would you use:

1   **id-dajaaj kaan laziiz fi9lan**

2   **b-aHibb il-mashwi il-mishakkal khuSuuSan**

3   **maa b-aHibb is-samak**

4   **b-aHibb il-laHma il-mashwiyya kitiir**

5   **b-afaDDil il-akl in-nabaati**

6   **maa b-aakul il-laHma abadan**

a   if you don't eat meat at all?
b   to say you prefer vegetarian food?
c   to say you especially like the mixed grill?
d   to say you don't like fish?
e   to say that the chicken was really delicious?
f   to say you like grilled minced meat a lot?

2   For each question circle the correct answer.

a   **b-tHibb is-samak?** na9am, <u>b-aHibbu</u>/<u>b-aHibbha</u> kitiir.
b   **b-taakul il-kufta?** laa', maa <u>b-aaklu</u>/<u>b-aakulha</u> abadan.
c   **b-tHibbi il-mujaddara?** laa', maa <u>b-aHibbu</u>/<u>b-aHibbha</u>.
d   **b-taakli ir-ruzz bi Haliib?** na9am, <u>b-aaklu</u>/<u>b-aakulha</u>.
e   **b-taakhud il-Hilu?** na9am, <u>b-aakhdu</u>/<u>b-aakhudha</u>.
f   **b-taakhud il-ba'laawa?** na9am, <u>b-aakhdu</u>/<u>b-aakhudha</u>.

3   Number the following phrases in the order you might hear them in a restaurant:

a   **biddna Taawila li itnayn.**   b   **haada kullu.**
c   **marhaba, kam shakhS?**   d   **itfaDDalu. ayy khidma?**
e   **ayy naw9 mashwiyyaat 9andkum?** f   **biddna itnayn kufta mashwiyya, min faDlik.**
g   **9andna kufta mashwiyya, wa samak mashwi, wa dajaaj mashwi il-yawm.**
                                       h   **biddak shi taani?**

now you're talking!

1 **2•79** Imagine you're in a restaurant on the Syrian coast with your friend who is a vegetarian. Ask the waiter for a table for two.

- **itfaDDalu.**
- ◆ Ask the waiter what type of vegetarian food he has.
- **9andnaa salaaTaat kitiir Tab9an.**
- ◆ Say OK and ask for one aubergine dip and one crushed wheat and parsley salad.
- **wa biddak mashwiyyaat?**
- ◆ Say you'll have one mixed grill.
- **HaDirtak biddak shi taani?**
- ◆ Say yes, you'd like more bread.
- **HaaDir.**

2 **2•80** You've just finished eating at a restaurant in Homs and the manager comes over to ask you how you found the food. You'll hear **in shaa' allaah** which means *God willing*.

- **ahlan wa sahlan, ana mudiir il-maT9am. kiif kaan il-akl?**
- ◆ Say that the food was really delicious.
- **kiif kaanat il-muqabbilaat?**
- ◆ Say the starters were delicious as well, especially the beans.
- **wa kiif kaanat il-khidma?**
- ◆ Say the service was excellent, and the waiter was very nice.
- **shukran kitiir. marra taanya in shaa' allaah?**
- ◆ Say yes, God willing.

quiz

1 Would **mujaddara** be suitable for a vegetarian?

2 At a restaurant, how would you say *We'd like a table for three*?

3 Which of the following is the odd one out and why? **kunaafa, mutabbal, tabbuuleh, falaafil, fuul.**

4 What does **kamaan khubz** mean?

5 Which adjective would you use to complete this phrase: **il-khidma kaanat** …… **laziiza/mumtaaza.**

6 How do you say *I never drink beer*?

7 How would you ask someone how the food was?

8 If **akalt** means *I/you* (m) *ate*, how would you ask *What did you eat yesterday*?

Now check whether you can …

- understand the Arabic for basic menu items
- ask for a table in a restaurant
- ask what kind of food is available in a restaurant
- order a meal
- say what you like, don't like and prefer
- pay a compliment on the food and service

Now get ready for the final Checkpoint, which covers the whole of **Talk Arabic**, with a bit of revision. Listen to the conversations again, test your knowledge of the key language by covering up the English and Arabic in turn, and use the quizzes and checklists at the end of each unit to assess how much you remember.

Checkpoint 3

You're on a tour of the Middle East and you've just arrived in Amman where you're meeting up with your friend, Khalid.

1   You have a booking at the Shepheard's Hotel in Amman for five nights. At reception which of the following would be the correct thing to say:

a   ahlan wa sahlan. Hajazt ghurfa hawn.
b   is-salaam 9alaykum. biddi ghurfa li khams layaali.
c   is-salaam 9alaykum. 9andi Hajz li khams layaali.
d   ahlan wa sahlan. 9andak ghurfa li khams layaali?
e   is-salaam 9alaykum. Hajazt khams ghuraf hawn.

2   2•81 Listen to the receptionist and make a note of the things she says to you:

1   ....
2   ....
3   ....
4   ....
5   ....

3   2•82 You visit Khalid in his office. Listen to him telling Nadia his travel plans for the week and note down what he's doing including when he'll be in Baalbek, Damascus, Beirut and London. Listen out for **abi** *my father* and **ummi** *my mother*.

Mon		**Fri**	
Tues		**Sat**	
Wed		**Sun**	
Thur			

4   **2.83** Listen to the following information, and write down where you are likely to be in each situation:

1 .... 2 ....

3 .... 4 ....

5 .... 6 ....

7 .... 8 ....

5   You go with Khalid to Damascus and while he's working you get ready to explore. How would you ask the receptionist:

a if you can use the internet?
b how to get to the Umayyad Mosque?
c where you can buy an English newspaper?
d if the National Museum is far from the hotel?

The receptionist gives you these directions to the Mosque: **ruuH 9ala Tuul, wa fi aakhir ish-shaari9 liff yamiin. khud taani yasaar. il-jaami9 il-umawi mi'aabil is-suu'**. Write them down in English.

....

....

....

6   After your visit to the Umayyad Mosque you go to a café in the Old City and get talking to a young man called Bilal sitting at the next table. What questions do you need to ask him to get these replies?

a ....
   • **b-atkallam ingliizi shwayya.**

b ....
   • **ana Taalib fi jaami9at dimashq.**

c ....
   • **laa', ana mish min dimashq, ana min Homs.**

d ....
   • **ana mish mitzawwij.**

e ....
   • **9andi itnayn wa 9ishriin sana.**

f ....
   • **laa', ana maa b-aHibb il-akl il-ingliizi.**

7   You offer Bilal a drink as he has given you some good advice for your trip tomorrow to Aleppo.

- Ask him what he would like to drink.
- **b-aakhud 9aSiir rumaan**.
- Ask the waitress for a mint tea for you and Bilal's juice.
- **itfaDDalu**.
- Ask for the bill.
- **miyya wa sittiin lira, min faDlak**.

How much change would you get from 200 Syrian pounds?

8   You're now at Damascus station trying to buy a second class return ticket to Aleppo. You need to find out what time the train leaves, and how long it takes. For each question choose the correct options.

a   **law samaHt, ayy saa9a b-yimshi/b-yuSal il-qiTaar il-jaay li Halab?**

b   **'addaysh b-taakhud/b-tiruuH ir-riHla min hawn li Halab?**

c   **biddi tazkarat ruuHa raj9a/ruuHa, daraja uula/daraja taanya, min faDlak.**

9   In Aleppo you visit its famous covered market where one of the vendors asks you if you would like to buy something from his stall.

Say the following to him:
- No thanks, I just want to look.
- Yes, the dish is pretty, but I have a lot of dishes.
- Can I have a look at the coffee pot?
- How much is it?
- No, that's very expensive. No way!
- How about 200 Syrian pounds?
- I'm sorry, that's a lot!

10 You've arranged to meet Bilal and some of his friends that evening for dinner. Tareq is from Beirut and is an accountant in Damascus, Sophie Lowry is a teacher from Edinburgh.

How would they answer these questions:
- **shuu ismak/ismik?**
- **min wayn inta/inti?**
- **shuu shughlak/shughlik?**

11 You're going to order for everyone, so make a note on the menu of who wants what:

Sophie would like: smoked aubergine dip, falafel, grilled fish, milk pudding.

Tareq would like: beans, mixed grill, baklava.

Bilal would like: rice with lentils, grilled lamb, rice pudding.

You would like: crushed wheat and parsley salad, grilled chicken, crème caramel.

How would you ask a waitress for sesame paste and more bread?

12 After an excellent visit to Damascus you get a taxi to the airport to fly back to London. Fill in the gaps in the conversation you have with the driver. **9al wa't** means *on time*.

- **mumkin .... il-maTaar law samaHt?**
- **itfaDDal.**
- **'addaysh .... min hawn lil-maTaar?**
- **ta'riiban .... waaHda. wayn raayiH HaDirtak?**
- **ana .... li London.**
- **kiif kaanat dimashq?**
- **................... mumtaaza. dimashq madiina ....**
- **aymta ....**
- **................... saa9atayn.**
- **in-shaa' allaah b-nuSal il-maTaar 9al-wa't!**
- **...................**

is–salaaTaat il–lubnaaniyya w–il muqabbilaat	السلطات اللبنانية والمقبّلات
mutabbal	متبّل
fuul	فول
falaafil	فلافل
tabbuuleh	تبولة
mujaddara	مجدرة

aTbaaq il–mashwiyyaat 9al–faHm	اطباق المشويات على الفحم
kufta mashwiyya	كفتة
kibda mashwiyya	كبدة
dajaaj mashwi	دجاج
samak mashwi	سمك
mashwi mishakkal	مشوي مشكّل

il–Hilu	الحلو
krim karamil	كريم كرامل
umm 9ali	أم علي
ba'laawa	بقلاوة
ruzz bi Haliib	رز بحليب
kunaafa	كنافة

in-shaa' allaah
b-yaakhud
saa9a
jamiila
taakhudni
ir-riHla
raayiH
ba9d
kaanat

mabruuk! *Congratulations!* You have now reached the end of **Talk Arabic**. **bit tawfii'fil musta'bal** *We wish you success in the future.*

transcripts and answers

This section contains the scripts of all the **Talk Arabic** conversations. Answers which consist of words/phrases from the conversations are in bold type; other answers are given separately.

Unit 1

Page 8

2 • **is-salaam 9alaykum.**
 ◆ wa 9alaykum is-salaam.
 • **kiif il-Haal?**
 ◆ bi-khayr il-Hamdullilaah.
 • **ahlan.**
 ◆ ahlan. kiif il-Haal?
 • il-Hamdullilaah.

3 • **ahlan wa sahlan** ya madaam Fawziyya.
 ◆ **ahlan fiik. kiif il-Haal?**
 • **bi-khayr, shukran. w-inti?**
 ◆ **il-Hamdullilaah.**

4 • **ahlan ya Mona.** kiif il-Haal?
 ◆ **bi-khayr, shukran. w-inta?**
 • il-Hamdulillaah.

Page 9

2 • **SabaaH il-khayr madaam Fawziyya.**
 ◆ SabaaH in-nuur.

 • **masaa il-khayr, aanisa Hoda.**
 ◆ ahlan, masaa in-nuur. kiif il-Haal?
 • bi-khayr, il-Hamdulilaah, w-inti?
 ◆ il-Hamdullilaah, bi-khayr, shukran.

 • **SabaaH il-khayr sayyid Hamdi.**
 ◆ SabaaH in-nuur.

 • **ma9a as-salaama sayyid Haddad.**
 ◆ allaah yisalmik.

3 • allaah yisalmak.
 • ma9a as-salaama. ashuufak ba9dayn.
 • allaah yisalmik.

• SabaaH il-khayr, kiif Haalak?
• ma9a as-salaama, ashuufik ba9dayn.
1 m; 2 m; 3 f; 4 m; 5 f

4 SabaaH il-khayr, ya Rania.
 allaah yisalmak.
 ashuufik ba9dayn.

Page 10

2 • **law samaHt, HaDirtak Lutfi?**
 ◆ laa', ana mish Lutfi, ana Jamal.
 • law samaHti, HaDirtik Zeinab?
 ◆ aywa, ana Zeinab.
 • ahlan wa sahlan, ya Zeinab.
 ◆ ahlan fiiki.
 • HaDirtak Nureddine?
 ◆ laa', ana mish Nureddine, ana Mustafa?
 • wa HaDirtik Samia?
 ◆ laa', ana mish Samia ana Nadia!
She's looking for Lufti, Zeinab, Nureddine, Samia.

3 • **law samaHt**, HaDirtak Mustafa Amin?
 ◆ **aywa**, ana Mustafa Amin, wa **HaDirtak**?
 • ana Adnan Hasan.
 ◆ ahlan wa sahlan. **ana** Mustafa Amin. **HaDirtik** Dalia Mustafa?
 • laa', **ana mish** Dalia Mustafa. ana Amira Ahmad.
 ◆ ahlan, ya Amira!

Page 11

2 • ahlan wa sahlan, **ismi** Sami Suleiman, **shuu ismik**?
 ◆ **ahlan fiik. ismi** Nadia Rif'at.
 • **tasharrafna.**
 ◆ **ish-sharaf ili.**
shuu ismak *is left over*

3 • ahlan wa sahlan, **shuu ismik**?
 ◆ **ismi** Zeinab, **w-inta**?
 • ismi Ahmad, **tasharrafna. shuu ismak**?
 ◆ ismi Farid.

- marHaba.
- marHabtayn.

4 • ahlan wa sahlan, ismi Omar. shuu ismak?
  ◆ ahlan fiik, ismi Sami.
  • marHaba Sami.
  ◆ marHabtayn. shuu ismik?
  • ismi Tara, tasharrafna.
  ◆ ish-sharaf ili. w-inta, shuu ismak?
  • ismi Abdu, kiif il-Haal?
  ◆ bi-khayr, il-Hamdullilaah.
  1 c, 2 a, 3 d, 4 b

Page 12

1 a 7; b 1; c 8; d 5; e 9; f 3; g 6; h 2; i 4

2 a SabaaH il-khayr/SabaaH in-nuur;
b masaa il-khayr/masaa in-nuur;
c is-salaam 9alaykum/wa 9alaykum
is-salaam; d ma9a as-salaama/allaah
yisalmik/yisalmak.

3 a ahlan ya Ahmad; b ahlan fiik;
c w-inti, kiif il-Haal?

Page 13

1 • masaa il-khayr.
  ◆ **masaa in-nuur**.
  • ahlan wa sahlan, ismi Nabiil. shuu ismik?
  ◆ **ahlan fiik, ismi Barbara**.
  • tasharrafna.
  ◆ **ish-sharaf ili**.

2 ◆ **tasharrafna. kiif il-Haal?**
  • bi-khayr, shukran. il-Hamdullilaah. wa HaDirtik?
  ◆ **bi-khayr, shukran.**
  • ma9a as-salaama. ashuufik ba9dayn.
  ◆ **allaah yisalmik**.

3 ◆ **ahlan wa sahlan.**
  • ahlan fiiki, ya Barbara.
  ◆ **ahlan, inta Mustafa?**
  • laa', ana mish Mustafa, ismi Mourad!

Page 14

1 in reply to is-salaam 9alaykum;
2 HaDirtik; 3 excuse me to a man, excuse
me to a woman; 4 morning; 5 ahlan wa

sahlan, marHaba, is-salaam 9alaykum;
6 shuu ismak? 7 ish-sharaf ili; 8 ashuufak
bukra.

Unit 2
Page 18

2 • ahlan, min wayn inta, ya George?
  ◆ ana min **lubnaan**.
  • inta min il-maghrib, ya Muhsin?
  ◆ laa', ana mish min il-maghrib. ana min **maSr**.
  • w-inta, ya Tareq?
  ◆ ana min **is-sa9uudiyya**.
  • min wayn inti, ya Nadia? inti min is-sa9uudiyya kamaan?
  ◆ laa', ana min **il-urdun**.
  • wa HaDirtik?
  ◆ ana ismi Ruba, ana min **suuriya**!
George: Lebanon; Muhsin: Egypt;
Tareq: Saudi Arabia; Nadia: Jordan; Ruba:
Syria

3 • ahlan wa sahlan. ismi Hasan Shoukry.
  ◆ ahlan fiik, ismi Mark Jones. ana min London. min wayn inta, ya Hasan?
  • ana min maSr.
  ◆ inta min il-qaahira?
  • laa', ana min **iskandariyya**.

4 min wayn inti, ya Farida?

Page 19

2 amriika, amriiki, amriikiyya;
iskutlanda, iskutlandi,
iskutlandiyya; fransa,
fransi, fransiyya; ingilterra,
ingliizi, ingliiziyya; irlanda,
irlandi, irlandiyya; maSr,
maSri, maSriyya; il-maghrib,
maghribi, maghribiyya; is-sa9uudiyya,
sa9uudi, sa9uudiyya; tuunis,
tuunisi, tuunisiyya; suuriya, suuri,
suuriyya

3 • Hussein, min wayn inta?
  ◆ ana **lubnaani**.
  • Maha, inti lubnaaniyya kamaan?
  ◆ laa', ana mish lubnaaniyya, ana **maghribiyya**.
  • Adam, inta amriiki?

- aywa, ana **amriiki**.
- Jacqueline, inti min fransa – inti fransiyya?
- aywa, ana **fransiyya**.
- David, inta min briiTaanya?
- aywa, min briiTaanya, ana **iskutlandi**.

Hussein: Lebanese; Maha: Moroccan; Adam: American; Jacqueline: French; David: Scottish.

Page 20

2
- wayn **saakna** fil-urdun, ya Nadia?
- ana saakna **fi** 9ammaan.
- w-inta ya MuHsin, **wayn** saakin?
- ana saakin **fil-qaahira**.
- inta **saakin** fil-qaahira kamaan, ya George?
- laa', ana **mish saakin** fil-qaahira, ana saakin fi bayruut.

3 sayyid Adnan min suuriya, bass huwwa saakin fi baghdaad. madaam Amira saakna fid-daar il-bayDa. sayyid Hussein min maSr, bass saakin fi Taraablus. sayyid Mustafa saakin fi jadda. madaam Lucy saakna fil jazaa'ir, bass hiyya briiTaaniyya.

1 e; 2 a; 3 c; 4 d; 5 b

Page 21

2 6, 9, 1, 3, 5, 8, 0, 2, 10, 4, 7

4
- raqm tilifawn il-maktab 0134 0460 wa raqm tilifawn il-bayt 0146 0179 wa raqm il-mubayl 0993 2271.

office: 0134 0460; home: 0146 0179; mobile: 0993 2271

5
- shuu raqm tilifawn il-maktab?
- raqm tilifawn il-maktab Sifr, waaHid, arba9a, arba9a, itnayn, sab9a, sab9a, sitta.
- 9andik mubayl?
- aywa, raqm il-mubayl Sifr, tis9a, tis9a, arba9a, sab9a, sab9a, tis9a, itnayn. wa raqm tilifawn il-bayt Sifr, waaHid, arba9a, arba9a, waaHid, sitta, sitta, khamsa.
- Tayyib. shukran.

office: 0144 2776; mobile: 0994 7792; home: 0144 1665

Page 22

1 *a* ana min maSr, saakin fil-qaahira. ana maSri.
b ana min il-maghrib, saakna fid-daar il-bayDa. ana maghribiyya.
c ana min is-sa9uudiyya, saakin fi jadda. ana sa9uudi.
d ana min suuriya, saakna fi dimashq. ana suuriyya.
e ana min iskutlanda, saakin fi Edinburgh. ana iskutlandi.

2 *a* tis9a, 9; *b* tamanya, 8; *c* arba9a, 4; *d* khamsa, 5

3 Lucy Abbott; ingilterra; ingliiziyya

4 il-maghrib: sitta; fransa: itnayn; tuunis: talaata: lubnaan: waaHid; iskutlanda: khamsa: suuriya: tis9a; maSr: arba9a; il-urdun: sab9a

Page 23

1
- min wayn inta?
- **ana min fransa. inta min il-urdun?**
- laa', ana min tuunis. wayn saakin?
- **saakin fi Paris. shuu ismak?**
- ismi Jamal, marHaba.

2
- inti min fransa kamaan?
- **laa', ana min briiTaanya**.
- wayn saakna?
- **saakna fi York**.
- shuu ismik?
- **ismi Louise**.

3
- raqm tilifawn il-bayt: Sifr, waaHid, tis9a, sitta, sitta, khamsa, tamanya

Jamal's home number is: 019 6658.

- **raqm il mubayl: Sifr, tis9a, sab9a, waaHid, arba9a, arba9a, khamsa, talaata, sab9a, sitta.**

Page 24

1 Saudi Arabia; 2 maghribi means Moroccan, the other two are countries; 3 ana min ingilterra, saakin (m)/saakna (f) fi London; 4 tamanya, 9ashara; 5 ana maSriyya; 6 huwwa min suuriya; 7 a woman; 8 shuu raqm tilifawn il-maktab?

Unit 3

2 ● haada jawzi, Sinaan.
  ◆ ahlan wa sahlan, ismi Ewan.
  ● ahlan fiik.
  ◆ wa haadi zamiilti Shahla.
  ● marHaba.
  ◆ marHabtayn, ana Ewan.
Sinaan is Farida's husband, Shahla is Farida's colleague.

3 ● haadi **marti** Layla.
  ◆ ahlan wa sahlan.
  ● ahlan fiik.
  ◆ wa haada **SaaHibi** Adnaan.
  ● marHaba, ya Adnaan.
  ◆ marHabtayn.
  ● wa **haadi SaaHibti** Marwa.
  ◆ tasharrafna.
Marwa is Shahla's friend.

4 *a* haadi marti Suzanne; *b* haada jawzi John; *c* haada zamiili Lutfi; *d* haadi SaaHibti Jamila.

2 ● inta mitzawwij, ya Nabiil?
  ◆ aywa, ana mitzawwij wa marti min amriika.
  ● 9andak awlaad?
  ◆ aywa, 9andi arba9 awlaad, ibn waaHid wa talaat banaat.
  ● w-inti, ya Hasna, inti mitzawwija?
  ◆ aywa, ana mitzawwija wa 9andi bint waaHda. w-inta, ya Mark?
  ● ana mish mitzawwij, wa maa 9andi awlaad.
Nabiil Shukri: married; Hasna Sabri: married; Mark Jones: not married.

3 *Nabiil Shukri: 1 son, 3 daughters; Hasna Sabri: 1 daughter; Mark Jones: no children.*

4 ● inti mitzawwija, ya Samia?
  ◆ aywa, ana mitzawwija.
  ● 9andik awlaad?
  ◆ 9andi talaat banaat. w-inti, ya Linda?
  ● **ana mish mitzawwija, wa maa 9andi awlaad.**

2 ● inta muhandis, ya Ewan?
  ◆ laa', ana mish muhandis, ana **Taalib** fil-jaami9a.
  ● inti Taaliba kamaan, ya Brigitte?
  ◆ laa', ana mish Taaliba, ana **mumarriDa**.
  ● w-inta, ya John?
  ◆ ana **muHaasib**.
  ● ya Hilary, shuu shughlik?
  ◆ ana **Tabiiba**.
  a 3; b 4; c 1; d 2

3 ● Ahmad Khaalid muHaasib fi maktab fi 9ammaan.
  ● Leila Muraad ustaaza fi jaami9at baghdaad.
  ● Mahmuud Saber Tabiib fi mustashfa fi Liverpool.
  ● Jumaana Dalaal mudarrisa fi madrasa fi iskandariyya, wa Salah Nazmi muhandis fi sharika amriikiyya.
Ahmad Khaalid: accountant in an office in Amman; Leila Muraad: lecturer at Baghdad university; Mahmuud Saber: doctor in hospital in Liverpool; Jumaana Dalaal: teacher in a school in Alexandria; Salah Nazmi: engineer in an American company.

4 shuu shughlak, ya Mark?

2 17, 11, 20, 12, 16, 15, 19

4 ● ya Mark, haada MuHammed.
  ◆ ahlan, ya MuHammed. 9andak kam sana?
  ● 9andi **tamanta9shar sana**.
  ◆ wa haada Hasan, wa haada George.
  ● ahlan wa sahlan, ismi Mark. 9andak kam sana, ya Hasan?
  ◆ 9andi **talata9shar sana**.
  ● w-inta, ya George?
  ◆ 9andi **arba9tashar sana**.
MuHammed 18: Hasan 13: George 14.

5 ● 9andik awlaad, ya Shahla?
  ◆ 9andi walad wa bint.
  ● il-walad shuu ismu?

- ◆ ismu Sinaan wa 9andu Hida9shar
  sana.
- ● wa shuu ism bintik?
- ◆ binti ismha Latifa.
- ● wa kam sana 9andha?
- ◆ 9andha khamasta9shar sana.

Latifa is older.

1 *a 3; b 4; c 6; d 5; e 1; f 2*

2 *a mitzawwij; b talaat awlaad;
   c arba9 siniin; d 9ashar siniin; e
   sab9ata9shar sana*

3 haadi marti, Saida. hiyya mudarrisa.
   haada SaaHibi, Ashraf. huwwa
   mitzawwij. huwwa muHaasib. haadi
   zamiilti Lina. hiyya mish mitzawwija.
   hiyya Tabiiba.

1 ● ahlan. min wayn inta?
   ◆ **min Manchester fi ingilterra.**
   ● shuu ismak?
   ◆ **ismi David.**
   ● haadi martak?
   ◆ **aywa, ismha Rachel.**
   ● shuu shuglak?
   ◆ **ana mudarris.**
   ● wa 9andak awlaad?
   ◆ **aywa, 9andi bint waaHda, ismha
     Alison.**
   ● kam sana 9andha?
   ◆ **9andha itna9ashar sana.**

2 ● **HaDirtak mitzawwij?**
   ◆ aywa, ana mitzawwij.
   ● **haadi martak?**
   ◆ aywa, ismha Hiba.
   ● **9andak awlaad?**
   ◆ 9andi ibn waaHid.
   ● **shuu ismu?**
   ◆ ismu Hussein.
   ● **kam sana 9andu?**
   ◆ 9andu tis9a9ashar sana.
   ● **huwwa fil madrasa?**
   ◆ laa', huwwa Taalib fi-jaami9at
     dimashq.

*1 a hospital; 2 bint waaHda wa ibn
waaHid; 3 sitta; 4 sana; 5 female student;
6 haadi SaaHibti, Rana; 7 female; 8 ana
mish mitzawwija; 9 maa 9andi mubayl.*

Unit 4

2 ● shuu b-tHibbi?
   ◆ biddi waaHid shaay bi Haliib.
     wa itnayn shaay biduun Haliib,
     wa talaata 'ahwa maZbuuT, wa
     waaHid 'ahwa biduun sukkar, min
     faDlak.

a 1; b 2; c 3; d 1

3 ● **shuu** b-tHibbi?
   ◆ min faDlak. biddi waaHid **'ahwa**
     wa waaHid **shaay**.
   ● **bi** sukkar aw **biduun** sukkar?
   ◆ shaay biduun sukkar, wa 'ahwa
     maZbuuT.
   ● HaaDir.

2 ● ayy khidma?
   ◆ ayy 9aSiir 9andak?
   ● fiih 9aSiir burtu'aan, wa 9aSiir
     manga, wa 9aSiir shammaam.
   ◆ biddi waaHid **9aSiir burtu'aan** wa
     itnayn **9aSiir shammaam**.
   ● HaaDir.
   ◆ aah…wa **'aniinat mayya
     ma9daniyya** min faDlak.
   ● HaaDir.
   ◆ law samaHt, 9andak biira?
   ● laa', maa fiih biira.

*Orange juice, melon juice, mineral water.
He asks if they have beer.*

3 ● marHaba.
   ◆ marHabtayn. 9andak 9aSiir
     tuffaaH?
   ● laa', maa 9andi. fiih 9aSiir manga
     wa 9aSiir lamuun.
   ◆ Tayyib, biddi waaHid 'ahwa min
     faDlak wa 9ilbat cola.
   ● HaaDir.

*She orders coffee and cola; because they
don't have any.*

4 law samaHti, biddi waaHid shaay bi Haliib, wa itnayn 'ahwa maZbuuT, wa waaHid 9aSiir tuffaaH, wa itnayn 9aSiir shammaam, wa waaHid 'aniinat mayya ma9daniyya, wa talaata biira, min faDlik.

2 • b-tishrabi shaay, ya Nadia?
 ◆ laa' shukran, maa biddi shaay. **b-ashrab 'ahwa**, min faDlak.
 • Tayyib. 9ashaanak ya Hasan, b-tHibb shaay aw 'ahwa?
 ◆ waaHid **shaay biduun sukkar** 9ashaani, min faDlak.
 • HaaDir.
Nadia: coffee; Hasan: tea without sugar.

3 • ahlan ya Nabiil! kiif il-haal?
 ◆ bi-khayr shukran. w-inta?
 • il-Hamdulillaah. shuu b-tishrab?
 ◆ ana b-aakhud 'ahwa bi Haliib, min faDlak.
 • biddak 'aniinat mayya kamaan?
 ◆ laa' shukran, maa biddi mayya, w-inta?
 • 9ashaani… b-aakhud 'ahwa bass.

2 9ishriin, talatiin, talaata wa talatiin, arba9iin, arba9a wa arba9iin, khamsiin, khamsa wa sittiin, tamanya wa saba9iin.
22 not mentioned.

3 sitta wa 9ishriin, talaata wa khamsiin, waaHid wa sittiin, arba9a wa saba9iin, sab9a wa saba9iin, waaHid wa tamaniin, tis9a wa tis9iin, miyya.

5 • il-Hisaab, min faDlak.
 ◆ Tayyib…il-'ahwa bi arba9iin lira, wa il-9aSiir bi khamsa wa talatiin lira. il-majmuu9 khamsa wa sab9iin lira min faDlak.
 • itfaDDal, shukran kitiir.
 ◆ 9afwan!
The coffee is 40 Syrian pounds, the juice is 35 Syrian pounds, total is 75 Syrian pounds.

6 • il-Hisaab, min faDlak.

• sitta wa talatiin lira min faDlik.
• itfaDDal arba9iin…wa khalli il-baa'i 9ashaanak.
• shukran kitiir.
The tip is 4 Syrian pounds.

1 *a* 5; *b* 1; *c* 2; *d* 4; *e* 3.

2 *1* talaata wa tis9iin; *2* tamanya wa saba9iin; *3* tis9a wa tamaniin; *4* itnayn wa talatiin; *5* talaata wa khamsiin; *6* arb9a wa 9ishriin.

3 *a one tea with sugar; b three orange juices; c two semi-sweet coffees; d lemon juice; e coffee and a bottle of mineral water.*

1 • ayy khidma?
 ◆ **biddi itnayn 'ahwa maZbuuT wa waaHid shaay, min faDlak.**
 • bi Haliib aw biduun Haliib?
 ◆ **bi Haliib.**
 • HaaDir.

2 • **il-Hisaab, min faDlak.**
 ◆ itfaDDali. saba9iin lira.
 • **itfaDDal tamaniin lira. khalli il-baa'i 9ashaanak.**
 ◆ shukran kitiir. ma9a as-salaama.
 • **allaah yisalmak.**

3 • ahlan. shuu b-tishrabi?
 ◆ **ahlan fiik. 9andak biira?**
 • laa', maa fiih biira. 9andi 9aSiir burtu'aan aw 9aSiir tuffaaH.
 ◆ **b-aakhud 9aSiir burtu'aan, min faDlak.**
 • itfaDDali.

1 9afwan; 2 bass; 3 88; 4 9andik 9aSiir rumaan? 5 min faDlak; 6 9ashaani; 7 biduun sukkar; 8 the bill.

Checkpoint 1

1 *a* ahlan wa sahlan; *b* ana bi-khayr shukran; *c* tasharrafna; *d* 9andak kam

sana?; e SabaaH il-khayr; f haadi marti; g wayn saakna?; h ana mish mitzawwij(a).

2 a SabaaH (the others are all drinks); b mubayl (the others are all professions); c mitzawwij (the others are all places); d tuunisiyya (others are male nationalities); e ukht (others are male relatives); f 9ilba (others are fruit); g sharika (others are people); h Tayyib (the others are all greetings).

3 a shuu ismak?; b 9andak kam sana?; c min wayn inta?; d wayn saakin?; e shuu shuglak?; f inta mitzawwij?; g 9andi awlaad?

4 • is-salaam 9alaykum, ana ismi Ahmad. ana maSri min il-qaahira.
  ◆ wa 9alaykum is-salaam. ismi Lutfi ana suuri min dimashq.
  • wa ana Naima. ana maghribiyya min ir-ribaaT.
  ◆ ahlan ya Naima, ismi Suhail. ana sa9uudi min ir-riyaaD.
  • wa ismi Nadia. ana lubnaaniyya min bayruut.
  ◆ ahlan fiiki. ismi Susan. ana ingliiziyya min Leeds.

Ahmad: maSri; Lutfi: suuri; Naima: maghribiyya; Suhail: sa9uudi; Nadia: lubnaaniyya; Susan: ingliiziyya.

5 • liibya - itnayn waaHid tamanya.
  ◆ il-maghrib - itnayn waaHid itnayn.
  • maSr - itnayn Sifr.
  ◆ il-imaaraat - tis9a sab9a waaHid.
  • lubnaan - tis9a sitta waaHid.
  ◆ suuriya - tis9a sitta talaata.
  • il-urdun - tis9a sitta itnayn.
  ◆ is-sa9uudiyya - tis9a sitta sitta.
1 218; 2 212; 3 20; 4 971; 5 961; 6 963; 7 962; 8 966

6 a ayy 9aSiir 9andak/ik?; b shuu b-tHibb/i?; shuu b-tishrab/i?; c bi Haliib aw biddun Haliib?; d fiih/9andak/ik 9aSiir lamuun?; e 9ashaanak/ik?

7 1 d; 2 i; 3 g; 4 j; 5 h; 6 a; 7 e; 8 c; 9 f; 10 b

8 • marHaba.
  ◆ marHabtayn.
  • ana ismi Lutfi, shuu ism HaDirtik?
  ◆ ismi Mona.
  • ahlan wa sahlan, ya Mona. min wayn inti?
  ◆ ana min ir-ribaaT fil maghrib, bass saakna fi London.
  • ana marti maghribiyya. ana min il-urdun. HaDirtik mitzawwija?
  ◆ laa', ana mish mitzawwija, bass 9andi SaaHib min ingilterra. 9andak awlaad?
  • 9andi ibn waaHid, ismu Hasan.
  ◆ wa kam sana 9andu?
  • khams siniin. wa shuu shughlik, ya Mona?
  ◆ ana Tabiiba fi mustashfa.
  • ana Tabiib kamaan!

Doctor, London, Jordanian, married, boyfriend, one son .

9 a khamsa wa khamsiin lira; b tis9a wa saba9iin lira; c arba9a wa tis9iin lira; d sitta wa tamaniin lira.

10 a biddi itnayn shaay; b 9ashaani waaHid cola; c 9ashaani waaHid 'ahwa; d b-aakhud itnayn 9aSiir shammaam; e b-aakhud talaata mayya; f biddi khamsa 'ahwa bi Haliib; g biddi arb9a 9aSiir burtu'aan; h b-aakhud waaHid shaay bi na9na9.

Unit 5

Page 50

2 suu'; maktab bariid; dukkaan; dakaakiin; bank; ba'aal; maqha internet; matHaf; suubermarket; fundu'; maHaTTa; jaami9

3 • fiih **maktab bariid** hawn, wa fiih **suu'**, wa fiih **bank**, wa fiih **dakaakiin kitiir**.

1 post office, 2 market, 3 bank, 4 many shops.

4 • law samaHti, mumkin ti'uuli li fiih maqha internet hawn?
  ◆ aywa, fiih maqha internet.
  • wa fiih suubermarket?
  ◆ aywa, fiih.

- fiih ba'aal hawn?
- laa', maa fiih.
- law samaHti, mumkin ti'uuli li fiih matHaf hawn?
- aywa, fiih matHaf.

internet café ✓; supermarket ✓; grocer's ✗; museum ✓

Page 51

2 • SabaaH il-khayr.
- SabaaH in-nuur.
- mumkin ti'uuli li wayn maktab il-bariid?
- maktab il-bariid mi'aabil il-fundu'.
- wa mumkin ti'uuli li wayn is-suu'?
- is-suu' fi wasT il-madiina.
- wa maqha il-internet?
- maqha il-internet janb il-madrasa.
- wa fiih maHaTTa hawn?
- aywa, fiih maHaTTa waraa il-jaami9.

A station; B post office; C internet café; D market.

3 • law samaHt, fiih matHaf hawn?
- aywa, fiih matHaf.
- mumkin ti'uul li wayn il-matHaf biZ-ZabT?
- il-matHaf ba9d il-jaami9, mi'aabil il-maHaTTa.
- shukran kitiir.

The museum is past the bank and opposite the station.

4 mumkin ti'uli li wayn il-matHaf biZ-ZabT?

Page 52

2 yawm il-aHad, yawm il-itnayn, yawm it-talaata, yawm il-arba9, yawm il-khamiis, yawm il-jum9a, yawm is-sabt

3 • law samaHt, is-suubermarket maftuuH aymta?
- is-suubermarket maftuuH kull yawm.
- w-iS Saydaliyya maftuuHa kull yawm kamaan?
- laa', hiyya maftuuHa min yawm il-itnayn li yawm is-sabt.
- maktab il-bariid maftuuH il-yawm?
- laa', huwwa ma'fuul il-yawm. il-yawm yawm il-jum9a. maktab il-bariid maftuuH min yawm il-aHad li yawm il-khamiis.

The supermarket is open every day; chemist's Mon-Sat; post office open Sun-Thurs.

4 Post office isn't open today because it's Friday.

5 • law samaHt, il-matHaf maftuuH **kull** yawm?
- il-matHaf **ma'fuul** il-yawm, bass huwwa **maftuuH** bukra.
- wi il-Hadii'a?
- il-Hadii'a **maftuuHa** kull yawm.

Page 53

2 is-saa9a arba9a
is-saa9a itnayn
is-saa9a sitta
is-saa9a Hida9ashar
is-saa9a tamanya

3 • law samaHt, ayy saa9a b-yiftaH il-matHaf?
- huwwa maftuuH min is-saa9a tis9a lis-saa9a arba9a.

- law samaHti, ayy saa9a b-yiftaH il-maT9am?
- b-yiftaH is-saa9a sitta.
- wa ayy saa9a b-yi'fil?
- b-yi'fil is-saa9a 9ashara.

- law samaHt, ayy saa9a b-tiftaH il-maHaTTa?
- b-tiftaH is-saa9a khamsa, wa b-ti'fil is-saa9a tis9a.

a 9.00–4.00; b 6.00–10.00; c 5.00–9.00.

4 law samaHt, ayy saa9a b-yiftaH is-suu'?

Page 54

1 *a 7; b 5; c 6; d 8; e 3; f 2; g 1; h 4*

2 *a* il-matHaf maftuuH min yawm it-talaata li yawm il-khamiis. b-yiftaH is-saa9a tis9a. b-yi'fil is-saa9a khamsa.

b iS-Saydaliyya maftuuHa kull
yawm. b-tiftaH is-saa9a tamanya.
b-ti'fil is-saa9a sab9a.

c il-ba'aal maftuuH min yawm
il-itnayn li yawm is-sabt. b-yiftaH
is-saa9a 9ashara. b-yi'fil is-saa9a
sitta.

1 ● **law samaHt. mumkin ti'uul li fiih
maqha internet hawn?**
   ◆ aywa, fiih maqha internet mi'aabil
il-bank.
   ● **wayn maT9am 9alaa' id-diin?**
   ◆ il-maT9am janb is-suu'.
   ● **shukran, ma9a as-salaama.**
   ◆ allaah yisalmak.

2 ● **law samaHti, ayy saa9a b-yiftaH
maktab il-bariid?**
   ◆ maktab il-bariid b-yiftaH is-saa9a
tamanya.
   ● **huwwa maftuuH kull yawm?**
   ◆ laa', huwwa ma'fuul yawm il-aHad.
   ● **il-matHaf maftuuH il-yawm?**
   ◆ laa', huwwa ma'fuul il-yawm.
il-matHaf maftuuH bukra.
   ● **shukran kitiir.**
   ◆ ahlan wa sahlan.

*1 yawm il-jum9a; 2 aymta, wayn;
3 maa fiih, maftuuH, b-yi'fil;
4 dakaakiin; 5 mi'aabil opposite;
6 waraa behind; 7 il-mustashfa;
8 maT9am il-fundu'.*

Unit 6

2 ● law samaHti, mumkin ti'uuli li kiif
aruuH lis-suu'?
   ◆ **huwwa 9ala Tuul, fi aakhir ish-
shaari9.**
   ● shukran kitiir.

*a It's straight ahead; b at the end of the
road.*

3 ● law samaHt, mumkin ti'uul li wayn
a'rab suubermarket?
   ◆ **aasif, maa b-a9raf.**

   ● law samaHti, mumkin ti'uuli li
wayn a'rab suubermarket?
   ◆ aywa, fiih suubermarket **fi taani
shaari9 9al-yasaar.**
   ● shukran kitiir.

*to the nearest supermarket; he doesn't
know; it's on the second street on the
left.*

4 ● **law samaHti, kiif aruuH lil-bank?**
   ◆ **huwwa fi awwal shaari9
9al-yamiin, fi aakhir ish-shaari9.**
   ● shukran kitiir.

*It's on the first street on the right, at the
end of the road.*

2 ● ruuHi li ishaarat il-muruur. liffi
yamiin. il-bank fi aakhir ish-
shaari9.
   ◆ ruuHi 9ala Tuul, liffi yasaar wa
ba9dayn khudi taani yamiin.
il-matHaf 9al-yamiin.
   ● ruuHi li ishaarat il-muruur, liffi
yamiin. khudi awwal yasaar. is-suu'
mi'aabil il-fundu'.

1 museum; 2 market; 3 bank

3 ● law samaHt, kiif aruuH lil-
jaami9a?
   ◆ liffi yasaar wa ba9dayn liffi yamiin,
khudi taani yamiin. il-jaami9a
fi awwal shaari9 9al-yamiin.

   ● law samaHti kiif aruuH lil-
jaami9a?
   ◆ liffi yasaar wa ba9dayn liffi yamiin.
khudi taani yasaar. il-jaami9a fi
aakhir ish-shaari9.

*The second person gave the right
directions*

1 miyya wa waaHid, miyya wa
itnayn, miyya wa 9ishriin, miyya
wa khamsiin, miitayn, talatmiyya,
arba9miyya, khamasmiyya,
sittmiyya, sab9amiyya, tamanmiyya,
tis9amiyya, alf, alfayn.

2 miyya wa talatiin, miitayn wa
khamsiin, khamasmiyya wa tamaniin,
sittmiyya wa arba9a wa talatiin,
sab9amiyya wa waaHid wa saba9iin,
tis9amiyya wa tis9a wa tis9iin.

4 • mumkin taakhudni li fundu'
   Cedarland, law samaHt?
   ◆ Ce-dar-land? **maa b-a9raf wayn
   haada-l fundu'.**
   ◆ huwwa fi shaari9 9abd il-9aziiz.
   ◆ fil Hamra?
   ◆ aywa, fil Hamra. il-fundu' ba9iid
   min hawn?
   • **ta'riiban talatiin da'ii'a.** … haadha
   shaari9 9abd il-9aziiz, ya akhi.
   ◆ Tayyib, il-Cedarland fi aakhir
   ish-shaari9 9al-yasaar, **Hawaali
   miitayn mitr** min hawn.
   • itfaDDal fundu' il-Cedarland!
   ◆ shukran kitiir.
*a he doesn't know where the hotel is;
b about 30 mins; c about 200m*

5 • law samaHt, fiih maqha il-internet
   hawn?
   ◆ aywa, fiih waaHid hawn.
   • huwwa 'ariib?
   ◆ **Hawaali khamasmiit mitr.**
   • shukran.
It's approx 500m away.

6 *a* is-suu' 'ariib min hawn?; *b* mumkin
taakhudni lil-jaami9a?

Page 63

2 • law samaHti, mumkin ti'uuli li
   wayn maHaTTat il-qiTaar?
   ◆ maHaTTat il-qiTaar? khud taani
   yamiin.
   • aasif, **mish faahim. marra taanya,
   min faDlik?**
   ◆ khud taani yamiin.
   • **mumkin titkallami shway shway,**
   min faDlik?
   ◆ aywa! khud … taani … yamiin.
   • shukran kitiir.
*b The railway station is on the second
right.*

3 • ahlan. min wayn HaDirtik?
   ◆ mumkin titkallam shway shway,

min faDlak?
   ◆ min wayn HaDirtik?
   ◆ HaDirtak b-titkallam ingliizi?
   • laa', b-atkallam 9arabi bass. ana
   min il-urdun. min wayn inti?
   ◆ aah! ana faahma! ana min amriika.
   ismi Sarah.
   • ahlan. ana ismi Abdallah.
   ◆ ahlan fiik! b-atkallam 9arabi
   shwayya.

Page 64

1 *a* 5; *b* 1; *c* 2; *d* 6; *e* 4; *f* 3

2 *a* ti'uul li; *b* a'rab; *c* aakhir; *d* 'ariib;
e taani; *f* taakhudni; *g* khamasmiit

3 • law samaHt, kiif aruuH lil-matHaf?
   ◆ ruuHi 9ala Tuul, ba9dayn khudi
   awwal shaari9 9al-yamiin.
   • mumkin marra taanya, min faDlak?
   ◆ ruuHi 9ala Tuul, ba9dayn khudi
   awwal shaari9 9al-yamiin.
   • huwwa ba9iid?
   ◆ laa', mish ba9iid. Hawaali
   arba9miit mitr min hawn.
   • shukran.
*To the museum; go straight on then take
the first road on the right; about 400m.*

Page 65

1 • **law samaHt, wayn a'rab bank?**
   ◆ ta'riiban miitayn mitr min hawn
   9al-yasaar.
   • **mumkin marra taanya min
   faDlak?**
   ◆ ta'riiban miitayn mitr min hawn
   9al-yasaar.
   • **shukran, ma9a as-salaama.**
   ◆ allah yisalmak.

2 • **law samaHti, HaDirtik
   b-tikallami ingliizi?**
   ◆ laa', maa b-atkallam ingliizi.
   • **kiif aruuH li maHaTTat il-qiTaar
   min hawn?**
   ◆ ruuHi 9ala Tuul, ba9dayn khudi
   taani shaari9 9al-yamiin, wa
   maHaTTat il-qiTaar fi aakhir ish-
   shaari9.
   • **asfa, mish faahma.**

- ruuHi 9ala Tuul, ba9dayn khudi taani shaari9 9al-yamiin.
- **Tayyib, ruuHi 9ala Tuul, ba9dayn khudi taani shaari9 9al-yamiin. hiyya ba9iida?**
- shwayya, mish ba9iida kitiir – ta'riiban kilomitr waaHid min hawn.
- **shukran kitiir.**
- 9afwan.

1 right; 2 ba9iid; 3 aruuH; 4 khamasmiit mitr 500m; 5 mumkin marra taanya, min faDlak; 6 slowly; 7 aasfa, maa b-a9raf; 8 I don't speak French.

Unit 7

2
- ahlan wa sahlan.
- ahlan fiiki.
- mumkin ashuuf haada-l isharb?
- aywa, itfaDDali.
- 9andak alwaan taanya?
- 9andi **aHmar** wa **akhDar** wa **abyaD**.
- 9andak **aSfar**?
- aasif. maa 9andi.
red, green, white, yellow

3
- marHaba. mumkin ashuuf haada-l 'amiiS, law samaHt?
- il-'amiiS il-aswad?
- aywa. mumkin a'iisu?
- Tab9an, itfaDDal.
- mmm… Saghiir shwayya. 9andak ma'aas akbar?
- laa', aasif, maa 9andi 'amiiS kibiir aswaD.
a false, he wants a black shirt; b true; c true.

4
- marHaba. mumkin ashuuf haadi-sh shanTa **iz-zar'a** min faDlik?
- itfaDDali.
- mmm, kibiira shwayya, wa maa b-aHibb il-lawn.
- Tayyib. b-tHibbi haadi-sh shanTa **il-Hamra**? itfaDDali. shuufi.

- laa', maa b-aHibb il-lawn **il-aHmar.**
- Tayyib, shuufi haadi-sh shanTa **il-khaDra**.
- aywa, haadi-sh shanTa il-khaDra Hilwa kitiir.
She likes the green handbag.

2
- law samaHti, 'addaysh **il-jakayt**?
- haada **bi khamsa wa arba9iin dinaar**.
- wa 'addaysh haadi-**l bluuza** iz-zar'a?
- haadi **bi talatiin dinaar**.
- Tayyib, 'addaysh haada?
- **il-fustaan bi miyya wa saba9iin dinaar**.
- haada ghaali kitiir!
- b-a9raf, haada l-fustaan min fransa!
- 9andik shi arkhas?
a 30 dinar; b 170 dinar; c 45 dinar.

3 The dress is from France.

4
- 'addaysh haadi-l jariida il-ingliiziyya?
- il-jariida bi tamaniin lira.
- wa 'addaysh haadi-l majalla?
- il-majalla bi tis9iin lira.
- 9andak kuruut?
- 9andi, hadawl bi 9ishriin lira.
- Tayyib. wa haada-l kitaab 'addaysh?
- haada bi miitayn lira.
- w-9andak Tawaabi9?
- mumkin tiruuH li maktab il-bariid.
- shukran.
a postcards; b English newspaper; c magazine; d book. Stamps aren't available; he must go to the post office.

5 haadi-sh shanTa ghaalya kitiir. 'addaysh hadawl il-kutub?

2
- fiih **tawaabil** mumtaaza hawn.
- laa' shukran. 9andi tawaabil kitiir fil-bayt.
- haadi-S **SuHuun** Hilwa.

- ◆ mumkin ashuufha? aywa, Hilwa kitiir.
- ● wi hawn fiih **Sawaani** Hilwa, wa **fanaajiin** mumtaaza kamaan.
- ◆ laa', maa biddi. laakin biddi **ibrii' shaay**.
- ● haada ibrii' shaay mumtaaz.
- ◆ mumkin ashuufu?
- ● itfaDDali.

3 ● mumkin ashuuf haada **ibrii' ish-shaay,** law samaHt?
- ◆ itfaDDali.
- ● 'addaysh haada?
- ◆ haada bi talaatmiit lira.
- ● haada ghaali kitiir. mumkin ashuuf haadi-S **Siniyya**, law samaHt?
- ◆ aywa. itfaDDali.
- ● 'addaysh haadi?
- ◆ haadi bi miitayn lira.
- ● Tayyib, b-aakhudha.
- ◆ biddik shi taani?
- ● bass iS-Siniyya. shukran.

teapot, tray. She buys the tray.

4 ● SabaaH il-khayr. mumkin ashuuf hadawl il-fanaajiin?
- ◆ itfaDDal. 'addaysh biddak?
- ● b-aakhud 9ashara min hadawl.
- ◆ Tayyib. wa biddak shi taani?
- ● mumkin ashuuf haada-S SaHn, law samaHt?
- ◆ 'addaysh biddak?
- ● biddi talaata, min faDlak.
- ◆ HaaDir. shi taani?
- ● aywa, 9andak ibrii' 'ahwa?
- ◆ itfaDDal.
- ● ana b-aHibbu. b-aakhdu.

10 cups, 3 dishes, one coffee pot.

Page 73

2 ● law samaHt, 'addaysh ibrii' il-'ahwa?
- ◆ bi talatmiyya wa khamsiin lira.
- ● haada ghaali kitiir. miitayn lira mniiH?
- ◆ laa', mish mumkin, aasif ya madaam.
- ● Tayyib, shuu aHsan taman 9andak?
- ◆ miitayn wa khamsa wa saba9iin lira.

- ● laa', laa' haada ghaali. itfaDDal miitayn wa khamsiin lira.
- ◆ HaaDir, 9ashaanik ya madaam, bi miitayn wa khamsiin lira.

a 350 Syrian pounds; b 250 Syrian pounds

3 **9ashaanik ya madaam** *for you madam*

4 ● itfaDDal, itfaDDal ya akhi. shuu biddak **tishtiri**?
- ◆ biddi **ashuuf** bass.
- ● haada-S SaHn jamiil kitiir.
- ◆ laa', shukran maa biddi **ashtiri.**
- ● iS-Siniyya bi miitayn lira bass!
- ◆ miyya wa khamsiin lira **mniiH**?
- ● laa', mish mumkin.
- ◆ shuu **aHsan** taman 9andak?
- ● miyya wa saba9iin lira.
- ◆ **b-aakhudha.**

Page 74

1 *a* Siniyya *tray, the rest are items of clothing; b* rakhiiS *cheap, the rest are used to make comparisons; c* miyya *a hundred, the rest are currencies; d* akbar *bigger, the rest are colours.*

2 *a* iz-zar'a; *b* il-aswad; *c* il-Hilwa; *d* kibiir; *e* il-aHmar; *f* akbar; *g* arkhaS; *h* mumtaaz.

3 *a* ashuufu; *b* ashtiri; *c* b-aakhudha; *d* haada-l; *e* b-aakhudha; *f* hadawl il-.

Page 75

1 ● ahlan, SabaaH il-khayr.
- ◆ **SabaaH in-nuur. 'addaysh haada-l 'amiiS il-abyaD?**
- ● il-'amiiS bi miyya wa 9ishriin lira.
- ◆ **mumkin a'iisu?**
- ● itfaDDal.
- ◆ **Saghiir shwayya. 9andak ma'aas akbar?**
- ● laa', maa 9andi.

2 ● marHaba, ahlan wa sahlan. itfaDDal.
- ◆ **law samaHti, 'addaysh haadi-sh shanTa?**
- ● haadi bi tis9amiit lira suuriyya.
- ◆ **9andik shanTa Hamra?**
- ● 9andi bass aswad wa azra'.

◆ **Tayyib, b-aakhud ish-shanTa iz-zar'a.**

3 ● aywa, ayy khidma?
◆ **mumkin ashuuf haadi-S Siniyya?**
● itfaDDal.
◆ **'addaysh haadi?**
● haadi bi miitayn lira.
◆ **haadi ghaalya kitiir. miyya wa 9ishriin mniiH?**
● laa', mish mumkin.
◆ **shuu aHsan taman 9andak?**
● miyya wa sittiiin kwayyis?
◆ **itfaDDal, miyya wa khamsiin lira**.
● Tayyib, itfaDDal.

Page 76

1 the dish is beautiful, the beautiful dish; 2 miitayn riyaal is more as it is 200 (itnayn riyaal is 2); 3 akbar; 4 aTwal; 5 colour; 6 biddi khamsa min hadawl; 7 aSghar 'amiiS; 8 Hamra; 9 b-aakhudha; 10 kuruut taanya.

Checkpoint 2

Pages 77–80

1 ● maT9am kebabji fi shaari9 il-Hamra mish ba9iid min hawn, Hawaali khamsa da'aayi' min il-fundu'.
● il-jaami9a il-amriikiyya 'ariiba kitiir min il-fundu' fi aakhir haada-sh shaari9! Hawaali khamasmiit mitr min hawn.
● il-matHaf il-waTani ba9iid shwayya min hawn, janb fundu' is-safiir, Hawaali 9ishriin da'ii'a min hawn bit-taksi.

a in il-Hamra street, not far from here, about 5 minutes from the hotel; b very near the hotel, at the end of the road, about 500m away; c quite far, next to Hotel is-safiir, about 20 minutes away by taxi.

2 ● maT9am kebabji maftuuH kull yawm min is-saa9a waaHda lis-saa9a Hida9sh.
● il-jaami9a il-amriikiyya maftuuHa min yawm il-itnayn li yawm il-jum9a.

● il-matHaf il-waTani ma'fuul kull yawm aHad.

maT9am kebabji: open every day from 1-11; il-jaami9a il-amriikiyya: open Mon–Fri; il-matHaf il-waTani: closed every Sun.

3 *a 6; b 7; c 1; d 5; e 4; f 9; g 10; h 8; i 3; j 2*

4 ibrii', finjaan, Siniyya; fustaan, isharb, 'amiiS; matHaf, maHaTTa, maktab bariid; 9ala Tuul, 9al yasaar, 9al yamiin; ruuH, liff, khud; miitayn, talatmiyya, arba9miyya; mi'aabil, janb, waraa.

5 *a 5; b 7; c 2; d 6; e 3; f 4; g 1*

6 ● **ibri il-'ahwa** bi sittmiyya wa khamsiin lira.
● **il-jariida il-ingiiziyya** bi miyya wa talatiin lira.
● **sitt fanaajiin** bi khamasmiit lira.
● **Siniyya 9arabiyya** bi saba9miit lira.
● **'amiiS** bi khamsmiyya wa talatiin lira.
● **il-isharb** bi talatmiyya wa arba9iin lira.

coffee pot 650 lira; English newspaper 130 lira; 6 cups 500 lira; Arabic tray 700 lira; shirt bi 530 lira; scarf 340 lira.

7 *a HaDirtak/HaDirtik b-titkallam/ b-titkallami ingliizi?; b mumkin ti'uul li/t'uulli li wayn a'rab Saydaliyya?; c il-maHaTTa 'ariiba min hawn?; d ayy saa9a b-yiftaH il-bank?; e 'addaysh haada?; f fiih suubermarket hawn?*

8 *1 ghaalya; 2 mniiH; 3 a'iis; 4 aHsan; 5 kiif; 6 liff; 7 khud*

9 ● law samaHti, mumkin ti'ulli li wayn il-maHaTTa il-kibiira?
◆ na9am – bass hiyya ba9iida shwayya. khud awwal yamiin wa ba9dayn ruuH 9ala Tuul wa khud taani shaari9 9al-yamiin. il-maHaTTa 9al-yasaar.
● shukran.

- law samaHt wayn fundu' riyaaD is-salaam?
- fundu' riyaaD is-salaam? mish ba9iid min hawn. liffi yasaar ba9dayn khudi awwal yamiin wa ba9ayn taani yamiin. w-il fundu' 9al-yasaar.
- shukran kitiir.

- wayn maktab il-bariid?
- maktab il-bariid? min Café France liffi yasaar, ruuHi 9ala Tuul wa maktab il-bariid 9al-yamiin mi'aabil il-qunSuliyya il-fransiyya.
- shukran.

- mumkin ti'uull li wayn is-suu'?
- na9am…is suu' waraa baab marraaksh.
- wayn baab marraaksh?
- shuuf! baab marraaksh mish ba9iid. ruuH yamiin wa ba9dayn khud taani shaari9 9al-yasaar wa baab marraaksh 9al-yamiin. is-suu' waraa baab marraaksh.

1 Hotel Riyaad salaam; 2 the market; 3 the post office; 4 the big station

10 *1 c; 2 d; 3 a; 4 b*

11 *a 2; b 1; c 3; d 3; e 2; f 1; g 3; h 1; i 2*

Unit 8

2 • marHaba!
- marHabtayn. 9andik ghurfa?
- li kam shakhS?
- li shakhSayn. **biddi ghurfa li shakhSayn bi Hammaam**, min faDlik.

- marHaba!
- marHabtayn. **biddi ghurfa li talaat ashkhaaS**, min faDlik.
- Tayyib. 9andi ghurfa **biduun Hammaam**.
- b-aakhudha. shukran.

- ahlan wa sahlan. 9andak ghurfa?
- ahlan fiik li kam shakhS?

- li shakhSayn. **biddi ghurfa li shakhSayn bi takyiif.**

- SabaaH il-khayr.
- SabaaH in-nuur.
- **biddi ghurfa li shakhS waaHid bi Hammaam**, min faDlik.

Double room with bathroom; room for three people without bathroom; double room with air-conditioning; single room with bathroom.

3 • Tayyib, il-ghurfa li shakhSayn bi Hammaam 'addaysh il-layla, law samaHti?
- **bi fuTuur bi talatmiit lira** il-layla.
- wa biduun fuTuur?
- **biduun fuTuur bi miitayn wa khamsiin lira.**

With breakfast 300 Syrian pounds, without 250 Syrian pounds.

2 • li kam layla, ya madaam?
- biddi anzil **layltayn**.

- aymta biddak tinzil?
- **min il-yawm li yawm it-talaata**.

- ya aanisa, biddik tinzili li kam layla?
- biddi anzil **haadi-l layla bass**.

3 • is-salaam 9alaykum. il-fundu' il-umawi … aloo.
- ahlan wa sahlan. biddi ghurfa li shakhS waaHid, min faDlik.
- li kam layla?
- biddi anzil layltayn, **min yawm waaHid sitta li talaata sitta.**
- aywa, fiih ghurfa. il-ism, min faDlak?

- is-salaam 9alaykum, il-fundu' il-umawi. ayy khidma?
- ahlan wa sahlan. 9andik ghurfa li shakSayn?
- aymta biddik tinzili?
- biddi il-ghurfa **haadi-l layla bass**.
- asfa, **il fundu' kullu maHjuuz**.

- is-salaam 9alaykum. il-fundu'
  il-umawi. ayy khidma?
- wa 9alaykum is-salaam. biddi
  ghurfa **min yawm arba9a tis9a li
  yawm sitta tis9a**. mumkin?
- aywa, mumkin.

*a 1–3 June; b just for tonight (hotel is
full); c 4–6 September.*

2 • ahlan wa sahlan. ana ismi Maryam
    Munir. 9andi Hajz.
  ◆ maa fiih Hajz bi ismik. Hajazti
    aymta?
  • Hajazt imbaariH.
  ◆ li kam shakhS?
  • **li shakhSayn.**
  ◆ li kam layla?
  • biddi anzil **talaat layaali.**
  ◆ biddik ghurfa bi Hammaam?
  • Tab9an!
  ◆ Tayyib, **imli il-istimaara**, min
    faDlik.
  • itfaDDal.
  ◆ itfaDDali il-muftaaH. **ghurfa raqm
    miitayn wa 9ashara.**
  • shukran.

*a double with bath; b three nights; c to
fill in the form; d 210.*

3 The receptionist didn't have a booking
  in her name.

4 • marHaba.
  ◆ marHabtayn. 9andi Hajz. **ismi
    Patrick Murphy.**
  • inta Hajazt ghurfa li shakhSayn,
    **min yawm itnaa9sh talaata li
    sitta9sh talaata?**
  ◆ aywa.
  • jawaaz safarak, min faDlak.
  ◆ itfaDDali.
  • Tayyib. **jawaaz raqm: Sifr,
    Sifr, khamsa, itnayn, khamsa,
    tis9a,sitta, arba9a. il-jinsiyya:
    irlandi.** itfaDDal il-muftaaH.
    HaDirtak fi **ghurfa raqm tis9a wa
    khamsiin, fiT Taabi' it-taalit.**
  ◆ shukran. law samaHti, wayn
    il-asinsiir?
  • **il-asinsiir mi'aabil il-maT9am.**
  ◆ shukran.

*Patrick Murphy, from 12 to 16 March,
passport no. 00525964, Irish, room 59.
a third floor; b opposite the restaurant.*

2 • SabaaH il-khayr.
  ◆ SabaaH in-nuur, ya aanisa
    Maryam. ayy khidma?
  • law samaHt, **mumkin tuTlub taksi
    9ashaani?**
  ◆ Tab9an mumkin. ayy khidma
    taanya?
  • aywa, **mumkin akhalli shanTati
    hawn?**
  ◆ akiid.

*a she wants him to call a taxi; b to leave
her suitcase; it means anything else?*

3 • ya madaam Campbell, itfaDDali
    il-Hisaab.
  ◆ **mumkin adfa9 bi haada-l kart?**
  • Tab9an mumkin.

  • ahlan, ya Hasan.
  ◆ ahlan, ya duktuur Rushdi.
  • **mumkin asta9mil Hammaam
    is-sibaaHa?**
  ◆ Tab9an, huwwa fiT Taabi' it-taalit.

  • law samaHt.
  ◆ aywa, ya sayyid Ramzi?
  • **mumkin akhalli shanTati hawn?**
  ◆ aywa, akiid.

  • ahlan wa sahlan, ya aanisa
    Buthayna. itfaDDali il-muftaaH.
  ◆ ahlan fiik. law samaHt. **mumkin
    ashuuf il-mudiir?**
  • laa', aasif. mish mumkin il-yawm.
    il-mudiir f-iskandariyya!

*Mrs Campbell: pay with this card;
Dr Rushdi: use the swimming pool; Mr
Ramzi: leave his suitcase; Miss Buthayna:
see the manager.*

4 Miss Buthayna's; the manager is in
  Alexandria.

1 *a 9andik ghurfa?; b bi takyiif?
  c biddi anzil haadi-l layla bass;*

d 9andi Hajz; *e* 'addaysh il-layla?;
f mumkin asta9mil Hammaan
is-sibaaHa?; *g* Hajazt imbaariH.

2 *a* shakhS waaHid; *b* shakSayn bi
Hammaam; *c* takyiif; *d* tuTlub taksi;
e asta9mil il-internet.

3 *a* yawm waaHid wa talatiin waaHid;
b yawm arba9a wa 9ishriin itna9sh;
c yawm khamsa talaata; *d* yawm
tamanya sab9a.

Page 87

1 • marHaba, ayy khidma?
  ✦ **9andak ghurfa?**
  • biddak tinzil li kam layla?
  ✦ **layla waaHda bass.**
  • li shakhS waaHid?
  ✦ **laa', li shakhSayn wa bi
    Hammaam, min faDlak.**
  • aywa, fiih ghurfa bi sab9iin dinaar
    il-layla.
  ✦ **bi fuTuur?**
  • aywa, bi fuTuur.

2 • SabaaH il-khayr.
  ✦ **SabaaH in-nuur.**
  • ayy khidma?
  ✦ **il-Hisaab, min faDlik.**
  • raqm il-ghurfa, law samaHt?
  ✦ **ghurfa raqm miitayn wa 9ashara.**
  • saba9iin dinaar, min faDlak.
  ✦ **mumkin adfa9 bi haada-l kart?**
  • aywa, Tab9an.
  ✦ **mumkin akhalli shanTati hawn
    lis-saa9a arba9a il-yawm?**
  • aywa, akiid. b-ashuufak ba9dayn.
  ✦ **ma9a as-salaama.**

Page 88
*1 ghurfa; 2 biddi anzil arba9 layaali;
3 yawm sab9a 9ashara; 4 the manager;
5 ghurfa bi takyiif; 6 mumkin tuTlub taksi
9ashaani; 7 fill in the form; 8 the key;
9 biddi ghurfatayn.*

Unit 9
Page 92

2 • law samaHt. biddi aruuH li

ba9albak. kiif mumkin aruuH min
hawn?
  ✦ HaDritak raayiH aymta?
  • raayiH bukra.
  ✦ mumkin tiruuH bil **baaS** wa
    mumkin taakhud **taksi** kamaan.
  • mumkin aakhud il-qiTaar?
  ✦ laa', mish mumkin. maa fiih
    qiTaaraat fi lubnaan!
*bus, taxi; there aren't any trains in
Lebanon.*

3 • SabaaH il-khayr.
  ✦ SabaaH in-nuur.
  • raayiH lil-maTaar bukra. mumkin
    aakhud il-baaS min hawn?
  ✦ laa', maa fiih baaS lil-maTaar.
    laazim taakhud taksi.
  • 'addaysh it-taksi min hawn lil-
    maTaar?
  ✦ Hawaali arba9iin dinaar.
  • haada ghaali kitiir!

4 biddi aruuH lil-matHaf; mumkin
aakhud il-baaS?

Page 93

2 • law samaHt, haada-l baaS b-yruuH
    lil-jaami9 il-umawi?
  ✦ laa', haada-l baaS lil-jaami9a.
  • Tayyib, ayy raqm baaS b-yruuH li-
    jaami9 il-umawi?
  ✦ laazim taakhdi baaS raqm itnayn
    wa 9ishriin.
  • 'addaysh b-yaakhud?
  ✦ Hawaali 9ashar da'aayi' bass.
  • wa fiih baaS min hawn lil-maTaar?
  ✦ na9am, fiih ya madaam.
  • ayy raqm?
  ✦ miyya.
*a true; b false, bus no. 22; c false, it takes
10 minutes; d false, bus no.100 goes to
the airport.*

3 • law samaHt, fiih baaS li Halab min
    hawn?
  ✦ aywa fiih.
  • 'addaysh b-yaakhud?
  ✦ **b-yaakhud Hawaali khams
    saa9aat.**
  • min wayn b-yruuH?
  ✦ min hunaak, 9al-yasaar.

- law samaHti, haada-l baaS b-yruuH li 9ammaan?
- aywa.
- 'addaysh b-taakhud ir-riHla?
- **ir-riHla b-taakhud Hawaali arba9 saa9aat.**
- wa 'addaysh b-taakhud ir-riHla li Homs?
- **Hawaali saa9atayn.**
- min wayn b-yruuH?
- min hunaak, 9al-yamiin.
- shukran, ya madaam.

a 5 hours; b 4 hours; c 2 hours

4 *Aleppo:* min hunaak, 9al-yasaar *from over there, on the left; Homs:* min hunaak 9al-yamiin *from over there, on the right.*

Page 94

2 • **biddi arba9 tazaakir li dimashq,** min faDlik.
- daraja uula aw daraja taanya?
- **daraja uula,** min faDlik.
- biddak tazkarat ruuHa aw ruuHa raj9a?
- **ruuHa bass,** law samaHti.
- biddak lil yawm?
- laa', **li bukra.**
- Tayyib. arba9 tazaakir ruuHa li dimashq daraja uula. **il-majmuu9 talaat alaaf wa khamasmiit lira min faDlak.**
- itfaDDali. wa min ayy raSiif?
- **raSiif raqm sitta.**
- shukran.

4 single first class tickets to Damascus for tomorrow. Total 3,500 Syrian pounds.

3 platform number 6

4 • biddi **tazkarat ruuHa lir-ribaaT,** min faDlak. 'addaysh it-tazkara?
- **khamsa wa 9ishriin dirham,** min faDlak.
- ----------------
- biddi **tazkartayn ruuHa raj9a lil-jadiida,** law samaHt.
- lil-jadiida? **khamsa wa arba9iin dirham.**
- ----------------

- **talaat tazaakir ruuHa li faas,** min faDlik.
- **miyya wa 9ishriin dirham.**
- shukran.
- ----------------
- **il-maTaar**, min faDlik.
- ruuHa aw ruuHa raj9a?
- **ruuHa bass,** law samaHt.
- **itnaa9shar dirham,** min faDlik.
- itfaDDal.

a 125 dirhams; b 45 dirhams; c 120 dirhams; d 12 dirhams.

Page 95

2 • law samaHt, ayy saa9a il-qiTaar li Tanja?
- il-qiTaar il-jaay **b-yimshi ba9d rub9 saa9a.**
- ya9ni **is-saa9a Hidaa9shar wa nuSS**?
- aywa, Hidaa9ashar wa nuSS.
- wa ayy saa9a b-yuSal Tanja?
- **is-saa9a arba9 illa rub9.**
- shukran.

a 11.30; b a quarter of an hour; c 3.45

3 • ayy saa9a il-qiTaar il-jaay li marraaksh?
- ba9d nuSS saa9a. **is-saa9a talaata wa 9ashara.**
- wa aymta b-yuSal li marraaksh?
- **b-yuSal is-saa9a sitta.**
- ----------------
- ya ukhti, il-qiTaar li Tanja b-yimshi ayy saa9a?
- **b-yimshi is-saa9a arba9a illa rub9.**
- wa aymta b-yuSal Tanja?
- **b-yuSal Tanja is-saa9a khamsa wa tult.**
- shukran.
- ----------------
- law samaHti, aymta il-qiTaar il-jaay lil-jadiida?
- il-jadiida? ba9d saa9a – **is-saa9a sab9a wa 9ashara. b-yuSal il-jadiida is-saa9a tis9a wa nuSS.**
- shukran.

Marrakesh 3.10, 6.00; Tangiers 3.45, 5.20; Al-Jadida 7.10, 9.30.

4 aymta il-qiTaar il-jaay lir-ribaaT?

1 *a* 2; *b* 5; *c* 6; *d* 1; *e* 4; *f* 3

2 *a* is-saa9a sab9a wa nuSS; *b* is-saa9a
waaHda illa rub9; *c* is-saa9a itnayn
wa rub9; *d* is-saa9a talaata wa nuSS
illa khamsa; *e* is-saa9a arba9 wa tult;
f is-saa9a 9ashara illa 9ashara.

3 *1* b-yuSal; *2* aakhud; *3* b-yimshi;
4; b-taakhud; *5* taakhdi; *6* tiruuH

4 *a* 6; *b* 4; *c* 5; *d* 2; *e* 3; *f* 1

1 • **fiih baaS li dimashq?**
   ◆ aywa, fiih baaS li dimashq kull
     yawm is-saa9a talaata.
   • **'addaysh b-taakhud ir-riHla?**
   ◆ ir-riHla b-taakhud Hawaali arba9
     saa9aat min 9amman li dimashq.
   • **'addaysh it-tazkara?**
   ◆ biddak tazkarat ruuHa aw ruuHa
     raj9a?
   • **biddi tazkartayn ruuHa bass, min
     faDlik.**
   ◆ Tayyib, haada khamsiin dinaar, min
     faDlak.
   • **itfaDDali.**
   ◆ shukran.

2 • **aymta b-yimshi il-qiTaar il-jaay
     li Halab?**
   ◆ b-yimshi is-saa9a tamanya wa
     nuSS.
   • **aymta b-yusal il-qiTaar Halab?**
   ◆ b-yuSal is-saa9a itnaa9sh wa nuSS.
   • **biddi tazkarat ruuHa raj9a.**
   ◆ daraja taanya aw daraja uula?
   • **daraja uula, min faDlak.
     'addaysh?**
   ◆ tamanmiit lira.
   • **'addaysh daraja taanya?**
   ◆ sittmiyya wa khamsiin lira.
   • **biddi tazkara waaHda – ruuHa
     raj9a daraja uula, min faDlak.**
   ◆ itfaDDal. riHla sa9iida.
   • **shukran. il-qiTaar b-yruuH min
     ayy raSiif?**
   ◆ raSiif raqm itnayn.

1 *8.40*; *2* riHla; *3* ruuHa raj9a daraja
taanya; *4* four o'clock and four hours;
5 next; *6* railway station; *7* tazkartayn;
8 You must take a taxi and You can take
a taxi.

Unit 10

1 • il-yawm min il-muqabbilaat
     9andnaa: tabbuuleh, wa fuul, wa
     mutabbal; wa min il-mashwiyyaat
     9andnaa dajaaj mashwi, wa kibda
     mashwiyya, wa samak mashwi
     wa kufta mashwiyya. lil Hilu
     9andnaa umm 9ali, wa kunaafa,
     wa ba'laawa il-yawm.
*Not mentioned: falaafil; mashwi
mishakkal, krim karamil, ruzz bi Haliib.*

2 • itfaDDali. shuu b-tHibbi?
   • **waaHid kufta mashwiyya wa
     waaHid samak mashwi**, law
     samaHt.
   • HaDirtik biddik muqabbilaat?
   ◆ mmm….ya Hiba, biddik
     muqabbilaat?
   ◆ aywa, aywa,Tab9an! biddi
     tabbuuleh, min faDlik.
   ◆ Tayyib, **waaHid mutabbal** wa
     waaHid tabbuuleh.
   • HaaDir, ya madaam.
*Farida orders 1 grilled meat, 1 grilled fish,
1 smoked aubergine dip and 1 crushed
wheat and parsley salad.*

3 • law samaHt, **9andkum krim
     karamil** il-yawm?
   ◆ laa', maa fiih.
   • Tayyib, **b-aakhud ba'laawa** min
     faDlak.
*She wants crème caramel, she orders
baklava.*

2 • ya Mark, b-tHibb il-falaafil wa-l
     kibbeh?
   ◆ **b-aHibb il-kibbeh**, bass **maa
     b-aHibb il-falaafil.**
   • Tayyib, b-taakul laHma?

- laa', **maa b-aHibb il-laHma**. ana maa b-aakul laHma abadan.
- b-tHibb is-samak il-mashwi?
- aywa, **b-aHibb is-samak**, b-aHibbu kitiir.
- wa b-tHibb il-ba'laawa?
- aywa, **b-aHibbha** Tab9an! bass **b-afaDDil il-kunaafa**.

falaafil ✗; *kibbeh* ✓; *laHma* ✗; *samak mashwi* ✓; *ba'laawa* ✓; *kunaafa* ✓.

3
- ya Jaqueline, **b-tHibbi** il-kufta il-mashwiyya?
- ya9ni, mish kitiir, **b-afaDDil** id-dajaaj.
- w-inta, ya David, **b-tHibb** il-kufta il-mashwiyya?
- laa', ana nabaati, maa b-aakul laHma **abadan**!
- Tayyib, **b-taakul** salaaTaat lubnaaniyya?
- Tab9an, **b-aHibbha** kitiir.

nabaati vegetarian.

Page 104

2
- ya garsawn!
- aywa ya ustaaz? shuu b-taakhud?
- biddi **itnayn dajaaj mashwi**, wa **waaHid kibda mashwiyya**, wa **talaata mashwi mishakkal**, law samaHt. aah, wa ayy naw9 akl nabaati 9andkum?
- fiih mujaddara.
- Tayyib, **waaHid mujaddara** kamaan.
- wa HaDirtak biddak muqabbilaat?
- aywa, biddi **arba9 mutabbal** wa **itnayn SalSat TaHiina**, law samaHt.
- Tayyib. waaHid mujaddara, itnayn dajaaj mashwi, waaHid kibda mashwiyya, wa talaata mashwi mishakkal, w-il muqabbilaat – arba9 mutabbal wa itnayn TaHiina.
- aywa maZbuuT. **mumkin kamaan khubz**, law samaHt?
- HaaDir, ya ustaaz.

dajaaj mashwi 2; kibda mashwiyya 1; mashwi mishakkal 3; mutabbal 4; SalSat TaHiina 2; mujaddara 1. He asks for more bread.

3
- ahlan wa sahlan.
- ahlan fiiki. biddna Taawila li itnayn.
- itfaDDalu.
- ya aanisa. mumkin il-lista, law samaHti?
- itfaDDalu.
- ya Khalid, **il-akl hawn kwayyis kitiir**. ana b-aakhud il-kufta!
- ana b-aHibb il-kufta kamaan, ya Nadia.
- Tayyib. itnayn kufta mashwiyya, min faDlik. ayy naw9 Hilu 9andkum?
- 9andnaa **ruzz bi Haliib** wa **ba'laawa**.
- 9andkum umm 9ali?
- laa', **maa 9andnaa umm 9ali il-yawm**.
- Tayyib, biddak ruzz bi Haliib, ya Khalid?
- maa biddi Hilu, shukran.
- biddik shi taani?
- **haada kullu.**
- HaaDir.

a She says that the food is very good. b She suggests ruzz bi Haliib (rice pudding) and ba'laawa. c There is no umm 9ali (milk pudding) today.
d haada kullu.

4 ayy naw9 fawaakih 9andkum?; biddi itnayn mashwi mishakkal, min faDlak; b-aakhud waaHid mutabbal wa waaHid mujaddara, min faDlak.

Page 105

2
- kiif kaan il-akl, ya Jacqueline?
- **il-akl kaan laziiz jiddan.**
- w-inta ya David, il-akl kaan kwayyis?
- il-akl kaan laziiz jiddan, **khuSuuSan is-samak**.
- **il khidma kaanat mumtaaza fi9lan!** shukran kitiir ya Farida.
- **biddik taakli hawn marra taanya?**
- Tab9an. b-aHibb il-akl il-lubnaani kitiir!

1 David especially liked the fish;
2 Jacqueline was impressed with the food

and the service; 3 Farida asks if she would like to eat here again.

3 • is-salaam 9alaykum ana mudiir il-maT9am.
  ◆ wa 9alaykum is-salaam.
  • kiif kaan il-akl?
  ◆ **il-akl kaan laziiz, shukran.**
  • **khuSuuSan il-laHma il-mashwiyya.**
  ◆ wa kiif kaanat il-khidma?
  • **il-khidma kaanat mumtaaza.**
  ◆ w-il garsawn?
  • **il garsawn kaan laTiif jiddan.**

4 il-akl kaan laziiz, khuSuuSan id-dajaaj il-mashwi.

Page 106

1 *a 6; b 5; c 2; d 3; e 1; f 4*

2 *a b-aHibbu; b b-aakulha; c b-aHibbha; d b-aaklu; e b-aakhdu; f b-aakhudha*

3 *a 2; b 8; c 1; d 3; e 4; f 6; g 5; h 7*

Page 107

• **biddna Taawila li itnayn.**
  ◆ itfaDDalu.
  • **ayy naw9 akl nabaati 9andkum?**
  ◆ 9andnaa salaaTaat kitiir Tab9an.
  • **Tayyib. biddi waaHid mutabbal wa waaHid tabbuuleh.**
  ◆ wa biddak mashwiyyaat?
  • **b-aakhud waaHid mashwi mishakkal, law samaHt.**
  ◆ HaDirtak biddak shi taani?
  • **mumkin kamaan khubz, law samaHt?**
  ◆ HaaDir, ya ustaaz.

2 • ahlan wa sahlan, ana mudiir il-maT9am. kiif kaan il-akl?
  ◆ **il-akl kaan laziiz fi9lan.**
  • kiif kaanat il-muqabbilaat?
  ◆ **il-muqabbilaat kaanat laziiza jiddan, khuSuuSan il-fuul!**
  • wa kiif kaanat il-khidma?
  ◆ **il-khidma kaanat mumtaaza, w-il garsawn kaan laTiif jiddan.**
  • shukran kitiir. marra taanya, in shaa' allaah?

◆ **aywa, in shaa' allaah.**

Page 108

1 yes; 2 biddna Taawila li-talaata; 3 kunaafa is the odd one out as it is a dessert, the others tend to be starters; 4 more bread; 5 mumtaaza; 6 maa b-ashrab birra abadan; 7 kiif kaan il-akl?; 8 shuu akalt imbaariH?

Checkpoint 3

Pages 109–112

1 *c*

2 • mumkin jawaaz safarak, min faDlak?
  • imla il-istimaara, law samaHt?
  • HaDirtak fi ghurfa raqm talatmiyya wa arba9ta9sh.
  • itfaDDal il-muftaaH.
  • ghurftak fiT-Taabi' it-taalit.

1 your passport please; 2 can you fill in this form please; 3 you're in room 314; 4 here's the key; 5 your room is on the 3rd floor.

3 • yawm it-talaata, bukra ya9ni, ana laazim aruuH lil-mustashfa ashuuf abi, wa ba9dayn biddi aruuH li ba9albak ashuuf ummi yawm il-arba9a.
  ◆ kam yawm biddak tinzil hunaak?
  • li yawmayn. yawm il-jum9a laazim aruuH li dimashq lish-shughl, bass layla waaHda.
  ◆ biddak tiruuH li landan min dimashq aw min bayruut?
  • min bayruut. 9andi Hajz yawm il-aHad li landan. b-aakhud taksi min dimashq li bayruut is-sabt.
  ◆ riHla sa9iida, ya Khalid.
  • shukran, ya Nadia.

Tues: see father in hospital; Weds: to Baalbek to see mother; Thurs: Baalbek; Fri: to Damascus on business; Sat: taxi Damascus – Beirut; Sun: fly to London.

4 • il-qiTaar li-Tanja b-yimshi ba9d nuSS saa9a.
  ◆ riHla raqm khamsa Sifr arba9 li

dubay b-tiruuH ba9d saa9a.
- biddak ghurfa bi Hammaam?
- aasfa, maa 9andnaa akl nabaati.
- Hammaam is-sibaaHa fiT-Taabi' il-awwal.
- biddak daraja uula aw daraja taanya?
- min wayn b-aakhud il-baaS li 9ammaan?
- il-maTaar ba9iid min haada-l fundu'. khud taksi – aHsan.

1 train station; 2 airport; 3 hotel reception; 4 restaurant; 5 hotel reception reception; 6 train station; 7 bus station; 8 hotel reception.

5 *a* law samaHt, mumkin asta9mil il-internet?; *b* law samaHt, kiif aruuH lil jaami9 il-umawi?; *c* law samaHt, wayn mumkin ashtiri jariida ingliiziyya?; *d* law samaHt, il-matHaf il-waTani ba9iid min il-fundu'?

Go straight on and at the end of the street turn right. Take the second left. The Ommayad Mosque is opposite the market.

6 *a* HaDirtak b-titkallam ingliizi?; *b* shuu shuglak?; *c* inta min dimashq?; *d* inta mitzawwij?; *e* kam sana 9andak?; *f* b-tHibb il-akl il-ingliizi?

7 ● shuu b-tishrab?
  ◆ law samaHti, biddi waaHid shaay bi na9na9 wa waaHid 9aSiir rumaan.
  ● il-Hisaab min faDlik.

You'd get 40 lira change.

8 *1* b-yimshi; *2* b-taakhud; *3* ruuHa raj9a, daraja taanya.

9 ● laa' shukran, biddi ashuuf bass.
  ● aywa, iS-SaHn Hilu bass 9andi SuHuun kitiir.
  ● mumkin ashuuf ibrii' il-ahwa?
  ● 'addaysh haada?
  ● laa', haada ghaali kitiir. mish mumkin!
  ● miitayn lira mniiH?
  ● aasif, haada kitiir!

10 ismi Tareq. ana min bayruut. ana muHaasib fi dimashq. ismi Sophie. ana min Edinburgh. ana mudarrisa.

11 Sophie: mutabbal, falaafil, samak mashwi, umm 9ali; Tareq: fuul, mashwi mishakkal, ba'laawa; Bilal: mujaddara, kufta mashwiyya, ruzz bi Haliib; You: tabbuuleh, dajaaj mashwi, kriim karamil.
law samaHti, biddi SalSat TaHiina wa kamaan khubz, min faDlik.

12 ● mumkin taakhudni lil-maTaar, law samaHt?
  ◆ itfaDDal.
  ● 'addaysh b-yaakhud min hawn lil-maTaar?
  ◆ ta'riiban saa9a waaHda. wayn raayiH HaDirtak?
  ● ana raayiH li London.
  ◆ kiif kaanat dimashq?
  ● kaanat mumtaaza. dimashq madiina jamiila.
  ◆ aymta **ir-riHla**?
  ● **ba9d** saa9atayn.
  ◆ in-shaa' allaah b-nuSal il-maTaar 9al-wa't!
  ● **in-shaa' allaah**.

grammar

G1 All Arabic **nouns** are either masculine or feminine. Nouns referring to people have the same gender (i.e. masculine or feminine) as the sex of the person. Nouns ending in **-a** are almost always feminine. Similarly most but not all nouns not ending in **-a** are masculine.

The gender of a noun affects adjectives and verbs, which must agree with (that is 'match') the noun in terms of taking a masculine or feminine form. (G7 adjectives; G9–G11 verbs)

G2 Unlike English, Arabic does not add **-s** for the **plural**.

Masculine nouns denoting professions and nationalities add **-iin** to the singular:

maSri- maSriyiin *Egyptian(s)*	lubaani- lubnaaniyiin *Lebanese*	mudarris- mudarrisiin *teacher(s)*	muhundis- muhandisiin *engineer(s)*	muHaasib muHaasibiin *accountant(s)*

The feminine versions add **-aat** to the singular. This is also how you form the plural of other nouns that end in **-a**, as well as a few that don't:

maSriyya- maSriyyaat *Egyptian(s)*	lubnaaniyya- lubaaniyyaat *Lebanese*	mudarrisa- mudarrisaat *teacher(s)*	maHaTTa- maHaTTaat *station(s)*	tilifawn- tilifawnaat *telephone*

It tends to be easier to learn the plural of all other nouns individually, although there are a number of patterns:

bayt – buyuut *house(s)* **SaHn-SuHuun** *dish(es)*
SaaHib- aSHaab *friend(s)* **walad-awlaad** *boys(s)*
fustaan-fasaatiin *dress(es)* **finjaan-fanaajiin** *cup(s)*
maktab-makaatib *office(s)* **madrasa-madaaris** *school(s)*
saakin-sukkaan *resident(s)* **Taalib-Tullaab** *student(s)*

G3 A/an, the
Arabic has no equivalent of the English *a/an*: **bayt** means *house* or *a house*.

The is **il**, which changes according to whether the noun starts with a sun or a moon letter (see list on page 16). Nouns which start with a moon letter keep **il**: **il-bayt** *the house*, **il-maktab** *the office*; nouns which start with a sun letter replace the **l** in **il** by that letter: **is-sayyaara** *the car*, **iT-Taawila** *the table*.

This/that

This/that is **haada** (masculine) and **haadi** (feminine). *These/those* is **hadawl**:

haada Ahmad. *This is Ahmad*; **haadi Miriam.** *This is Miriam.*
hadawl mudarrisiin. *These are teachers.*

In sentences like *This book is expensive*, you have to include the definite article **il**, which changes to **l** in the singular only:
haada-l kitaab ghaali. *This book is expensive*; **haadi-l madiina jamiila.** *This city is beautiful*; **hadawl iT-Tullaab fransiyiin.** *These students are French.*

5 Possession is expressed by adding an ending onto a noun rather than by using a separate word like *my, your, their* etc.:

-i *my*	**-ak** *your* (m)	**-ik** *your* (f)	**-u** *his*
-ha *her*	**-na** *our*	**-kum** *your* (pl)	**-hum** *their*

bayt *house*: **bayti** *my house*; **baytu** *his house*
ism *name*: **ismak** *your (m) name*; **ismha** *her name*

If a noun ends in **-a**, this is replaced by **-t** before adding the possessive ending: **madrasa** *school*, **madrasti** *my school*
sayyaara *car,* **sayyaartik** *your* (to f) *car*

6 Arabic has no equivalent of the English *'s* for possession. *A manager's office* is simply **maktab mudiir**, or lit. *office manager.* *The manager's office* is **maktab il-mudiir**, with **il** going with the second noun rather than the first; lit. *office the manager.*

If the first noun ends in **-a**, then **-t** is usually added:
sayyaarat mudiir *a manager's car,* **sayyaarat il-mudiir** *the manager's car*

This construction is known in Arabic as the **Idaafa**.

7 **Adjectives** in Arabic normally come after what they describe. They agree in gender (masculine or feminine) and number (singular or plural) with the noun they describe.

If the noun is feminine singular, then the adjective has **-a** at the end:
masculine sing **bayt jadiid** *a new house* **maktab kibiir** *a big office*
feminine sing **sayyaara jadiida** *a new car* **madrasa kibiira** *a big school*

All plural nouns which refer to things rather than people behave as feminine singular:
buyuut jadiida *new houses* **makaatib kibiira** *big offices*

For people, the plural ending of the adjective is often the same as the ending used for nouns denoting professions and nationalities (G2):
awlaad maSriyiin *Egyptian boys* **banaat maSriyaat** *Egyptian girls*

If a noun is used with **il** *the*, then the adjective also takes **il**:

il-bayt il-abyaD *the White House*, **is-sayyaara il-jadiida** *the new car*

Without **il** in front of the adjective, these would mean *The house is white*, *The car is new*. (G15 'to be'; page 71 comparatives and superlatives)

G8 Personal pronouns, *I, you, he, she, it* etc. are not generally needed with verbs except for emphasis. They're used most often when there's no verb in the sentence, and in particular when English uses *am, is, are* which have no equivalent in Arabic:

ana min ingilterra. *I am from England*; **huwwa mudarris.** *He is a teacher.*

ana	*I/I am*	**iHna**	*we/we are*
inta/inti	*you/you are* (m/f)	**intu**	*you/you are* (pl)
huwwa	*he/he is*	**hum**	*they/they are*
hiyya	*she/she is*		

G9 Verbs

Arabic has two main tenses: the present and the past. There is no equivalent of the infinitive e.g. *to drink*. Verbs are normally listed in the third person masculine (*he*) of the past and present tense. The verb *to drink* is presented as **sharib/yishrab** *he drank/he drinks*.

G10 The present tense is formed by placing a prefix onto the front of the verb stem. You find the stem by removing the prefix from the masculine singular (**huwwa**). This prefix is a **y** followed by a helping vowel (usually **i**):

	drink	*go*	*see*	*speak*
ana	a̱shrab	a̱ruuH	a̱shuuf	a̱tkallam
inta	ti̱shrab	ti̱ruuH	ti̱shuuf	ti̱tkallam
inti	ti̱shrabi	ti̱ruuHi	ti̱shuufi	ti̱tkallami
huwwa	yi̱shrab	yi̱ruuH	yi̱shuuf	yi̱tkallam
hiyya	ti̱shrab	ti̱ruuH	ti̱shuuf	ti̱tkallam
iHna	ni̱shrab	ni̱ruuH	ni̱shuuf	ni̱tkallam
intu	ti̱shrabu	ti̱ruuHu	ti̱shuufu	ti̱tkallamu
hum	yi̱shrabu	yi̱ruuHu	yi̱shuufu	yi̱tkallamu

In addition to the prefix, the feminine singular *you* adds the ending **-i**, while the feminine plural *you* and *they* both add **-u**.

In some dialects, including Levantine, an extra **b-** is added at the beginning of the verb. Its use differs slightly from region to region but it always denotes a present tense:

b-ashrab shaay kull yoom. *I drink tea every day.*
b-tishrabi 'ahwa? *Do you* (f) *drink coffee?*

This **b-** prefix is not used with **laazim** *must* and **mumkin** *can* (G17):
mumkin titkallam shway shway? *Can you speak more slowly?*

There's no equivalent of the infinitive (the 'to' form of the verb) in Arabic. Instead, the corresponding form of the present tense is used:
biddi aruuH *I want to go*, lit. *I want I go*
biddu yiruuH *He wants to go*, lit. *he wants he goes*

11 Unlike the present tense, the **past tense** adds a suffix onto the end of the stem. Verbs are grouped, depending on how the spelling of their stem changes, into Sound, Hollow/Middle Weak, Final Weak and Doubled. The majority of verbs in Arabic are in the Sound group.

Verb type	Sound	Hollow	Final weak	Doubled
	booked	*was/were*	*walked*	*liked*
ana	Hajazt	kunt	mashayt	Habbayt
inta	Hajazt	kunt	mashayt	Habbayt
inti	Hajazti	kunti	mashayti	Habbayti
huwwa	Hajaz	kaan	masha	Habb
hiyya	Hajazat	kaanat	mashat	Habbat
iHna	Hajazna	kunna	mashayna	Habbayna
intu	Hajaztu	kuntu	mashaytu	Habbaytu
hum	Hajazu	kaanu	mashu	Habbu

2 Spoken Arabic often uses **active participles** instead of a verb. They have three forms: masculine singular (*I, you, he*), feminine singular (*I, you, she*) and plural (*we, you, they*).

They often indicate that an action is currently going on, rather like the English *-ing* ending (e.g. *I am learning Arabic*):

saakin *I'm/you're/he's living* **raayiH** *I'm/you're/he's going*
saakna *I'm/you're/she's living* **raayHa** *I'm/you're/she's going*
saakniin *we/you/they're living* **raayHiin** *we/you/they're going*

wayn saakin? *Where are you living?/Where do you live?*
wayn raayiH bukra? *Where are you going tomorrow?*

G13 Passive participles describe the state something is in: *open, closed, booked, broken*. They behave like adjectives and agree with the noun: **il bank maftuuH**. *The bank* (m) *is open*; **il madrasa maftuuHa.** *The school* (f) *is open.*

G14 The imperative is the form of the verb used to give instructions or advice: _turn_ *right*, _sit_ *down*, _take_ *two pills with water*. It has three endings depending on whether you're addressing a man, a woman or a group of people. Imperatives are formed by removing any prefix from the present stem and adding the following endings:

<u>b-</u>**yishuuf** *he sees, he looks*   **shuuf!** *look* (to m)

                                         shuufi! *look* (to f)

                                         shuuf<u>u</u>! *look* (to pl)

Sometimes -**i** is added to help with pronunciation:
<u>b-</u>**yishrab** *he drinks*   **ishrab!** *drink* (to m)

G15 There's no verb to be; spoken Arabic does not use *am, are, is*. The presence of the verb *to be* is assumed if there's nothing else acting as a verb in the sentence:
il-akl laziiz. *The food is delicious.* Lit. *the food delicious.*

But you do need the words for *was/were* when talking about the past:
il-akl <u>kaan</u> laziiz *the food <u>was</u> delicious*

fiih means both *there is* and *there are:*
fiih mayya. *There is water*; **fiih buyuut.** *There are houses.*

G16 There's no verb to have. Instead possessive endings (G5) are added to **9and.**

9andi *I have*   **9andak/ik** *you have* (m/f)   **9andu/ha** *he/she has*
9andi bayt fi bayruut. *I have a house in Beirut.*

bidd to want/need works in the same way:
biddi *I want/I'd like*   **biddak/biddik** *you want/you'd like* (m/f)

G17 **mumkin** can and **laazim** must don't change to agree with the person, but the verb that follows them does (G10):
mumkin ashuuf? *Can I see?*
laazim tishuuf iT-Tabiib. *You must see the doctor.*

G18 Negatives. There are two negative words: **maa** and **mish**.
maa negates verbs as well as *have, want, there is/there are*:
maa b-atkallam 9arabi. *I don't speak Arabic.*
maa 9andi bayt fi bayruut. *I don't have a house in Beirut.*
maa biddi ashrab shaay. *I don't want to drink tea.*
maa fiih maTaa9im hawn. *There aren't any restaurants around here.*

mish negates active and passive participles, adjectives and sentences without a verb:

binti <u>mish</u> saakna fi Edinburgh. *My daughter doesn't live in Edinburgh.*
il-bank <u>mish</u> maftuuH il-yawm. *The bank isn't open today.*
bayti <u>mish</u> kibiir. *My house isn't big.*
ana <u>mish</u> muhandis. *I'm not an engineer.*

19 **Object pronouns**, e.g. *it*, *him*, *them* are attached to the end of the verb. The ending you use depends on the gender of the noun it is replacing:
mumkin ashuuf<u>ha</u>? *Can I see her/it (f)/them (things)?*
mumkin taakhd<u>u</u>? *Can you take him/it (m)?*

20 **Numbers** (pp 21, 31, 41, 60, 62) follow varying rules when with a noun:
- **waaHid** *1* usually comes after what it refers to and has a feminine as well as masculine form: **ibn waaHid** *one son*; **bint waaHda** *one daughter*.
- **itnayn** *2* is rarely used when referring to two items (apart from when ordering food and drinks). Instead, the suffix **-ayn** is added to the singular of the noun: **baytayn** *two houses*; **yawmayn** *two days*. If the word ends in **-a** then the suffix is **-tayn**: **sanatayn** *two years*; **sayyaaratayn** *two cars*. This structure is known as the dual in Arabic.
- Numbers 3-10 go before the noun, which is in the plural. The numbers lose their **-a**: **arba9 kutub** *four books*; **khams fanaajiin** *five cups*.
- Numbers over 10 go before the noun, which is in the singular: **9ishriin kitaab** *twenty books*; **arba9iin yawm** *forty days*.
- Numbers 11-19 add **-ar** before the noun: **Hidaashar kitaab** *eleven books*; **khamastaashar Taalib** *fifteen students*.
- With *how many*, the noun is in the singular: **kam sana 9andak/ik?** *How old are you? lit. How many year do you have?*

The main exception to the above rules is when ordering items of food and drink, when the numbers are in their countable form and the noun is in the singular. For example:
itnayn 'ahwa *two coffees*; **talaata shaay** *three teas*

1 Arabic has a **root system**, with the majority of words made up of three root letters or radicals in the same order. Once you know the combination of radicals for a particular concept then you can build your vocabulary relating to this concept. For example, the radicals **k - t - b** denote the concept of writing:

kitaab *book*; **kutub** *books*   **kaatib** *writer*; **kuttaab** *writers*
katabt *I wrote*; **b-aktub** *I write*   **maktab** *office*; **makaatib** *offices*
maktaba *library*; **maktabaat** *libraries*   **maktuub** *written, letter*

Arabic–English glossary

This glossary contains the words found in this book, with their meanings in the context used here. Verbs are given without the b- prefix. Abbreviations: (m) masculine, (f) feminine, (s) singular, (pl) plural.

9

9afwan you're welcome
9ala Tuul straight ahead
9alaykum on/upon you
9al wa't on time
9al-yamiin on the right
9al-yasaar on the left
9andak/9andik you have (m/f)
9andi I have
9ammaan Amman
9andu/9andha he has/she has
9arabi Arabic; Arab (m)
9ashaanak/9ashaanik for you (m/f)
9ashaani for me
9aSiir juice
9ilba/9ilab can (s/pl)

A

a9raf I know
aakhdu/aakhudha I'll take it/them (m/f)
aakhir end, last (*final*)
aakul I eat
aanisa Miss, waitress
aasif/asfa I'm sorry (m/f)
ab father
abadan never
abyaD/bayDa white (m/f)
adfa9 I pay
aghla more/most expensive
aHibb I like
aHjiz I book
ahlan hi, hello
ahlan fiik/ahlan fiiki *reply* hello (to m/f)

ahlan wa sahlan hello, welcome
aHmar/Hamra red (m/f)
aHsan better, best
akbar bigger, biggest; larger, largest
akhalli I leave (*something*)
akhDar/khaDra green (m/f)
akh/ikhwa brother (s/pl)
akiid certainly
a'iisu/a'iisha I try it on (m/f)
akl food
allaah yisalmak/yisalmik *reply* goodbye (to m/f) *lit.* may God bless you
alwaan/lawn colours (pl/s)
amriika America
amriiki/amriikiyya American (m/f)
ana I/I am
ana faahim/ana fahma I understand (m/f)
ana mish I'm not
anzil I stay
a'rab nearer, nearest
arkhaS cheaper, cheapest
aruuH I go
aSfar/Safra yellow (m/f)
aSghar smaller
ashtiri I buy
ashuufak/ashuufik I see you (to m/f)
asinsiir/aninsiiraat lift (s/pl)
asta9mil I use
aswad/sawda black (m/f)
atkallam I speak

aw or
awlaad/walad children (pl/s)
awwal first
aymta when?
aywa yes
ayy khidma? Can I help you?
ayy naw9? What/Which kind of?
ayy saa9a What time?
azra'/zar'a (m/f) blue

B

ba9d after, past, beyond
ba9dayn later, afterwards
ba9iid/ba9iida far (m/f)
ba'aal grocer's
baab/abwaab door, gate (s/pl)
baaS/baaSaat bus (s/pl)
baghdaad Baghdad
ba9albak Baalbek
ba'laawa baklava
balad/buldaan country (s/pl)
banaat daughters
bank/bunuuk bank (s/pl)
bass but
bayDa/abyaD white (f/m)
bayruut Beirut
bayt/buyuut house (s/pl)
betinjaan maHshi stuffed aubergines
bi with *things*
biddak/biddik you want? (to m/f)
biddi I want/I would like
biddi ashtiri I want to buy

biddi ashuuf I want to look
biduun without
biira beer
bi-khayr well
bint/banaat daughter (s/pl)
biZ-ZabT exactly
bluuza/bluuzaat blouse (s/pl)
briiTaanya Britain
briiTaani/briiTaaniyya British (m/f)
b-titkallam/b-titkallami you speak (to m/f)
bukra tomorrow
burtu'aan orange
bukra tomorrow

D

da'ii'a/da'aayi' minute (s/pl)
dajaaj chicken
daraja taanya second class
daraja uula first class
dawli international
dhahaab departures
dimashq Damascus
dinaar *currency in Algeria, Bahrain, Iraq, Jordan, Kuwait, Libya and Tunisia*
dirham *currency in Morocco and UAE*
dukkaan/dakaakiin shop (s/pl)
duktuur/dakaatra doctor (s/pl)

F

faahim/faahma understand (m/f)
faas Fez
fanaajiin/finjaan cups (pl/s)
fawaakih fruit
fi9lan really, indeed
fi aakhir at the end

fi awwal in/on the first
fiih there is/there are
finjaan/fanaajiin cup (s/pl)
fransa France
fransi/fransiyya French (m/f)
fukhaar earthenware
fundu/fanaadi' hotel (s/pl)
fustaan/fasaatiin dress (s/pl)
fuTuur breakfast
fuul beans

G

garsawn waiter (aanisa waitress)
ghaali/ghaalya expensive (m/f)
ghurfa/ghuraf room (s/pl)
ghurfa raqm room number
gineeh pound *currency*
gineeh isterliini pound Sterling
gineeh maSri Egyptian pound

H

haada/haadi this (m/f)
haada kullu. That's all.
HaaDir OK
Habb il-haal cardamom
hadawl these, those
Hadii'a/Hadaayi' park (s/pl)
HaDirtak/HaDirtik *formal* you (m/f)
Hajz reservation
Hajazt I booked
Hajazt/Hajazti you booked (to m/f)
Halab Aleppo
Haliib milk
Hammaam bathroom
Hammaam is-sibaaHa the swimming pool
Hamra/aHmar red (f/m)

Hawaali about, roughly
hawn here
Hida9sh eleven
Hilu/Hilwa pretty (m/f)
Hilu dessert
Hisaab/Hisaabaat bill (s/pl)
hiyya she/she is
hulanda Holland
hunaak over there
huwwa he/he is

I

ibn/abnaa' son (s/pl)
ibrii' shaay/'ahwa tea/coffee pot
id-daar il-bayDa Casablanca
iftaH/iftaHi open *instruction* (to m/f)
ikhwa/akh brothers (pl/s)
il-Hamdullilaah praise be to God
il-imaaraat The Emirates
il-jadiida Al-Jadida
il-jazaa'ir Algiers, Algeria
il-maghrib Morocco
il-qaahira Cairo
il-urdun Jordan
il-yawm today
ila to, towards
illa except
imbaariH yesterday
ingilterra England
ingliizi/ingliiziyya English (m/f)
in shaa' allaah God willing
inta *informal* you/you are (m)
inti *informal* you/you are (f)
irlanda Ireland
irlandi/irlandiyya Irish (m/f)
ir-ribaaT Rabat
ir-riyaaD Riyadh
ishaarat il-muruur the traffic lights
isharb scarf

ish-sharaf ili *reply* the pleasure is mine
iskandariyya Alexandria
iskutlanda Scotland
iskutlandi/iskutlandiyya Scottish (m/f)
ism name
ismak your name (to m)
ismi my name
ismik your name (to f)
is-sa9uudiyya Saudi Arabia
is-salaam 9alaykum may peace be upon you
istimaara/istimaaraat form (s/pl)
itfaDDal/itfaDDali here you are; come this way; be my guest (to m/f)
iT-Taabi' il-awwal the first floor

J

jaami9/jawaami9 mosque (s/pl)
jaami9a/jaami9aat university s/pl)
jaay next
jadda Jeddah
jakayt/jakaytaat jacket (s/pl)
jamiil/jamiila beautiful (m/f)
janb near
jariida/jaraa'id newspaper (s/pl)
jawaaz raqm passport number
jawaaz safar passport
jawzi my husband
jiddan very
jinsiyya nationality

K

kaan he/it was
kaanat she/it was
kaas/kaasaat glass (s/pl)
kam? How many?
kamaan as well; another

kart/kuruut postcard (s/pl)
khaDra/akhDar green (f/m)
khidma service
khubz bread
khud/khudi take *instruction* (to m/f)
khuSuuSan especially
kibiir/kibiira big, large (m/f)
kiif how
kiif il-Haal? How are you?
kilomitr kilometre
kitaab/kutub book (s/pl)
kitiir many, a lot; very
kull every, all, whole
kull yawm every day
kunt I was/you were (m)
kuruut postcards
kushk kiosk
kwayyis good

L

laa' no
laakin but
laazim one must, should
laHma meat
lamuun lemon
laTiif/laTiifa nice (m/f)
lawn/alwaan colour (s/pl)
law samaHt/law samaHti excuse me; please (to m/f)
layla/layaali night (s/pl)
laziiz/laziiza delicious (m/f)
li to
liff/liffi turn *instruction* (to m/f)
liibya Libya
lira pound *currency*
lira suuriyya Syrian pound *currency*
lista menu
lubnaan Lebanon
lubnaani/lubnaaniyya Lebanese (m/f)

M

ma9a as-salaama goodbye
maa don't
maa 9andi I don't have
maa b-a9raf I don't know
maa biddi I don't want
ma'aas/ma'aasaat size (s/pl)
madaam Mrs
madiina/mudun town, city (s/pl)
madiinti my town, my city
madrasa/madaaris school (s/pl)
madrasat il-awlaad the boys' school
ma'fuul/ma'fuula closed (m/f)
maftuuH/maftuuHa open (m/f)
maghribi/maghribiyya Moroccan (m/f)
maHaTTa/maHaTTaat station (s/pl)
maHaTTat il-baaSaat the bus station
maHaTTat il-qiTaar the train station
maHjuuz booked, reserved
majalla/majallaat magazine (s/pl)
majmuu9 total
makaan il-iqaama the place of residence
maktab/makaatib office (s/pl)
maktab bariid post office
maktab isti9laamaat tourist information office
manga mango
maqha/maqaahi café (s/pl)
maqha internet internet café
marHaba hello
marHabtayn *reply to*

marHaba *lit. two hellos*
marraaksh Marrakesh
marra taanya again, a
second time
marti my wife
masaa evening
masaa il-khayr good
evening
masaa in-nuur *reply*
good evening
mashwiyyaat charcoal-
grilled food
masjid/masaajid mosque
(s/pl)
maSr Egypt
maSri/maSriyya
Egyptian (m/f)
maT9am/maTaa9im
restaurant (s/pl)
maTaar/maTaaraat
airport (s/pl)
matHaf/mataaHif
museum (s/pl)
mayya water
mayya ma9daniyya
mineral water
maZbuuT semi-sweet
(*for coffee*)
mazza mezze
mi'aabil opposite
min from
min faDlak/faDlik please
(to m/f)
min hawn from here
mish not
mish ba9iid/ba9iida It's
not far away (m/f)
mish faahim/faahma I
don't understand (m/f)
mish mumkin it's not
possible
mitzawwij/mitzawwija
married (m/f)
mitr metre
mniiH OK
mubayl mobile
mudarris/mudarrisa/
mudarrisiin teacher
(m/f/pl)

mudiir/mudiira manager
(m/f)
muftaaH/mafaatiiH key
(s/pl)
muhandis/muhandisa
engineer (m/f)
muHaasib/muHaasiba
accountant (m/f)
mumarriD/mumarriDa
nurse (m/f)
mumkin it is possible,
can
mumkin adfa9? Can I
pay?
mumkin a'iisu/a'iisha?
Can I try it on? (m/f)
mumkin aruuH? Can
I go?
mumkin ashuuf ...? Can I
have a look at ...?
mumkin titkallam/
titkallami? Can you
speak? (to m/f)
mumtaaz/mumtaaza
excellent (m/f)
muqabbilaat starters
mustashfa/
mustashfayaat hospital
(s/pl)

N

na9am yes
na9na9 mint
nabaati vegetarian
nuSS half
nuSS saa9a half an hour

Q/'

qiTaar/qiTaaraat train
(s/pl)
qunsuliyya consulate
'addaysh how much is/
are
'ahwa coffee
'amiiS/'umSaan shirt
(s/pl)
'aniina bottle
'ariib/'ariiba close by
(m/f)

R

raayiH/raayHa going
(m/f)
raSiif/arSifa platform
(s/pl)
riHla/riHlaat journey,
trip, flight (s/pl)
rakhiiS cheap
raqm/arqaam number
(s/pl)
riHla sa9iida bon voyage
riyaal *currency in Saudi
Arabia, Qatar and Oman*
rub9 quarter
rub9 saa9a a quarter of
an hour
rumaan pomegranate
ruuH/ruuHi go
instruction (m/f)
ruuHa single (ticket)
ruuHa raj9a return
(ticket)
ruzz rice

S

SaaHib/SaaHiba/
aSHaab friend (m/f/pl)
SaaHibi/SaaHibti my
friend (m/f)
saakin/saakna am living/
lives (m/f)
SabaaH morning
SabaaH il-khayr good
morning
SabaaH in-nuur *reply*
good morning
Safra/aSfar yellow (f/m)
Saghiir/Saghiira small
(m/f)
SaHn/SuHuun large dish
(s/pl)
salaaTa/salaaTaat salad
(s/pl)
SalSat TaHiina sesame
paste
samak fish
sana/siniin year (s/pl)
sawda/aswad black
(f/m)

Saydaliyya/saydaliyyaat chemist's (s/pl)
sayyaara/sayyaaraat car (s/pl)
sayyid Mr
shaari9/shawaari9 road, street (s/pl)
shaay tea
shakhS/ashkhaaS person/people
shakhSayn two people
shakhS waaHid one person
shammaam melon
shanTa/shunaT bag (s/pl)
sharika/sharikaat company (s/pl)
shi taani anything else
shughl work, business (noun)
shukran thank you
shuu what
shuuf/shuufi look (to m/f)
shway/shwayya a little, slowly
Siniyya/Sawaani tray (s/pl)
sukkar sugar
suu'/aswaa' market (s/pl)
suubermarket supermarket
Suura/Suwar photograph, picture (s/pl)
suuriya Syria
suuri/suuriyya Syrian (m/f)

T

Taabi9/Tawaabi9 postage stamp (s/pl)
taakhud it takes (f)
taakhudni you take me (to m)
taakul/taakli you eat (m/f)
Taalib/Taaliba/Tullaab student (m/f/pl)
taani/taanya second; other (m/f)
Taawila/Taawilaat table (s/pl)
Tab9an certainly, of course
Tabiib/Tabiiba/aTibbaa' doctor (m/f/pl)
taksi/taksiyaat taxi (s/pl)
takyiif air-conditioning
taman/atmaan price (s/pl)
Tanja Tangiers
Taraablus Tripoli
ta'riiban almost, roughly
tasharrafna pleased to meet you
tawaabil spices
Tayyib fine, OK
tazkara/tazaakir ticket (s/pl)
tazkara ruuHa single ticket
tazkara ruuHa raj9a return ticket
tazkartayn two tickets
tHibb/tHibbi? would you like? (m/f)
tilifawn/tilifawnaat telephone (s/pl)
tinzil/tinzili you stay (to m/f)
tishrab/tishrabi you (m/f) drink
ti'uul li/ti'uuli li tell me/ say to me (to m/f)
tuffaaH apple
Tullaab/Taalib students (pl/s)
tult a third
tuTlub/tuTlubi you order (m/f)
tuunis Tunisia, Tunis
tuunisi/tuunisiyya Tunisian (m/f)

U

ukht/ikhwaat sister (s/pl)
umm/ummahaat mother (s/pl)
urduni/urduniyya Jordanian (m/f)
ustaaz/ustaaza lecturer (m/f)
utiil/utiilaat hotel (s/pl)

W

wa and
wa 9alaykum is-salaam and upon you be peace
waaHid/waaHda one (m/f)
walad/awlaad child/ children
waraa behind
waTani national
wasT centre, middle
wayn where
wi and
w-inta/w-inti? and you? (to m/f)
wuSuul arrivals

Y

ya *before a person's name*
yaakhud it takes (m)
ya9ni I/you mean
yamiin right
yasaar left
yawm day
yi'fil/ti'fil it closes (m/f)
yiftaH/tiftaH it opens (m/f)
yimshi it departs (m)
yishrab he drinks
yuSal it arrives (m)

Z

zamiil/zamiila colleague (m/f)
zamiili/zamiilti my colleague (m/f)
zar'a/azra' blue (f/m)
ziyaada extra